D. A. Ellis

Grand Army of the Republic

History of the Order in the U. S. by Counties

D. A. Ellis

Grand Army of the Republic
History of the Order in the U. S. by Counties

ISBN/EAN: 9783337134266

Printed in Europe, USA, Canada, Australia, Japan

Cover: Foto ©ninafisch / pixelio.de

More available books at **www.hansebooks.com**

Grand Army of the Republic.

HISTORY OF THE ORDER IN THE U. S. BY COUNTIES.

✦ Otsego ✦ County ✦ Posts ✦

Department of New York,

Including a complete record of Soldiers surviving and buried in the County, with Company and Regiment,

TOGETHER WITH

Valuable Statistics & Miscellaneous Matter.

"I propose to fight it out on this line if it takes all Summer."—U. S. GRANT

COMPILED BY D. A. ELLIS.

Press of Historical Publishing Co.
1892.

MAJ.-GEN. JOHN A. LOGAN,
THE MOST DISTINGUISHED NAME IN THE ANNALS OF THE G. A. R.,
AND THE ORIGINATOR OF MEMORIAL DAY.

INTRODUCTORY

THIS little volume is offered to the Comrades of the Grand Army of the Republic in the County of Otsego in response to repeated suggestions that the names of the members of the order, together with the history of each Post, might be brought together for reference and for preservation in some enduring form. The original suggestion has been somewhat amplified, and a complete history of the Order, from its inception in 1866 to date, has been included, while there has been added certain valuable statistics and miscellaneous matter to supply piquancy and interest to the monotonous detail of the facts and figures indespensible to a satisfactory presentation of the work as originally begun.

It has been a labor of fraternal and interested love throughout many weeks, a number of things having conspired to delay its completion. The figures and tables of statistics have been compared and reverified with original Department and other reports, and it is hoped the book is reasonably free from inexcusable errors.

The few select advertisers, whose love for the soldier and whose disinterested generosity have made the publication of this little volume possible, are most heartily recommended to your favor.

HISTORY

OF THE

GRAND ARMY OF THE REPUBLIC.

By Past Commander-in-Chief George S. Merrill.

One of the most powerful organizations of the country is the Grand Army of the Republic.

This noble order, born in the stirring and bitter days that followed the close of the war, saw its first struggles for recognition extremely hard. Politics leaked into the organization, leading to its practical dismemberment. But it was again set on its feet, "Fraternity, Charity and Loyalty" were made its watch words, politics were excluded from the Order, and it has grown marvelously until, to-day, its noble work is felt in every section of the country—from the metropolitan city down to the smallest hamlet.

ITS ORIGIN.

Dr. Benjamin Franklin Stephenson, of Springfield, Ill., Surgeon of the Fourteenth Illinois Infantry, must be regarded as the father of the organization. Soon after his return from the seat of war, he conceived the idea of banding together, into a common brotherhood, the survivors of the awful conflict; and, communicating his idea to Chaplain W. J. Ruttlege, of the same regiment, the two went to work to perfect an organization. Others were invited into the work, and, in the early part of 1866, a ritual for the proposed order, prepared by Stephenson, was printed in the Decatur Tribune. This attracted the attention of about a dozen Decatur veterans to whom, under date of April 6th, 1866, a charter was granted; constituting Post 1. Stephenson's name was signed to the charter as Department Commander. The men whom Stephenson had first interested with others, in June, 1866, organized as Post 2, of Springfield, the charter list including 27 names. The work of organizing new posts now began and was rapidly pushed forward, and the Order extended into Indiana, Kansas, Minnesota, Missouri, Iowa, Pennsylvania, Ohio, Kentucky, Arkansas, Massachusetts, New York, Maryland and Wisconsin. July 12th the Department of Illinois was formed, with Gen. John M. Palmer as Commander. Dr. Stephenson, assuming the position as Acting Commander-in-Chief, issued a call for the first National Convention, to meet in Indianapolis Nov. 20th, 1866. Two hundred and twenty-eight delegates were entitled to representation, coming from the Departments of Iowa, Indiana, Illinois, Kansas, Kentucky, Wisconsin, Ohio, New York, Pennsylvania, Missouri and the District of Columbia, all of these States having organized Departments, formed since the first of July. At this meeting Gen. S. A. Hurlbut was chosen Commander-in-Chief of the G. A. R., he being the first one elected to the office. From this out the organization enjoyed a phenominal growth, but nothing like exactness as to the membership can be learned. No reports or records were made, but it is presumed that it at one time reached 200,000. In January, 1868, the second National Encampment was held in Philadelphia. It was not a very enthusiastic assemblage, as may be inferred when it is stated that the receipts for the preceding year were but $352, while the expenditures amounted to $1,637, leaving an indebtedness of $1,285. **The next year showed an increasing indebtedness, and this continued until 1872, when, for the** first time, a cash balance appeared in the Quarter-Master-General's hands. During these years Illinois and Indiana lent no assistance financially to the National body.

A FALLING OFF.

In 1869, owing to the adoption of unpopular laws, the membership of the organization fell off, and the enthusiasm of the remaining members waned in a corresponding degree. For years the order was enveloped in the deepest gloom, and the increase in membership, between 1871 and 1878, was but 992, the total membership in the latter year being 31,016. In 1879 the increase was somewhat larger and things again began to brighten up. The organization underwent a new birth in 1880, and since then has made rapid strides. Each year it has been more successful, and to-day it stands at the highest point of success.

The annual reports submitted to the recent National Encampment show that the Grand Army is steadily increasing in numbers and works of mercy. Its membership was never so large as it is now, and its charities are commensurate with the organization.

While it is true that more than $140,000,000 are annually paid to pensions to the disabled soldiers of the war of the Rebellion, those who are addicted to vulgar denunciation of the Union veterans as "pension grabbers" and "subsidy beggars," will do well to exercise self restraint. The fact that the organization has expended, during the last year, $261,350.18 for the relief of 28,419 cases, is an adequate vindication of its character. The Grand Army is not to be compared to blind Belisarius, standing at the doors of a national capitol and asking alms, but rather to the Good Samaritan, binding up the wounds and pouring in oil.

WHAT IT IS.

The Grand Army is, in itself, the most conspicuous and

convincing monument of patriotism and loyalty which the world possesses. Despite the inroads of death upon its ranks—more than 7,600 in 1889—it presents an enrollment approaching, if not exceeding, half a million of the survivors of the grandest army the world has ever seen—an army of freeman, who, upon the call of their country, forsook everything that was dear to them, animated alone by a spirit of loyalty to liberty and devotion to the flag. During nearly a quarter of a century it has endeavored to cherish the memories of the great struggle; to broaden the channels of charity; to deepen the sentiment of loyalty, and, through the tender services of Memorial Day, inculcate lessons of gratitude and awaken anew the sympathies and patriotic impulses of the people. It is banded together with no purpose of politics or thirst for power, welcoming all who were among the Nation's defenders, demanding no vows of allegiance except to the country and the flag, asking no pledges except those of fraternity, charity and loyalty.

COMMANDER-IN-CHIEF,

JOHN M. PALMER.

NEW YORK.

LIST OF PAST COMMANDERS-IN-CHIEFS,

GRAND ARMY OF THE REPUBLIC.

Commander.	State.	Elected.
S. A. Hurlbut,	Illinois,	Nov. 20, 1866.
John A. Logan,	Illinois,	Jan. 15, 1868.
John A. Logan,	Illinois,	May 12, 1869.
John A. Logan,	Illinois,	May 11, 1870.
A. E. Burnside,	Rhode Island,	May 10, 1871.
A. E. Burnside,	Rhode Island,	May 8, 1872.
Charles Devens,	Massachusetts,	May 14, 1873.
Charles Devens,	Massachusetts,	May 13, 1874.
J. F. Hartranft,	Pennsylvania,	May 12, 1875.
J. F. Hartranft,	Pennsylvania,	June 13, 1876.
J. C. Robinson,	New York,	June 26, 1877.
J. C. Robinson,	New York,	June 4, 1878.
William Earnshaw,	Ohio,	June 17, 1879.
Louis Wagner,	Pennsylvania,	June 8, 1880.
G. S. Merrill,	Massachusetts,	June 18, 1881.
Paul Vandervoort,	Nebraska,	June 21, 1882.
R. B. Beath,	Pennsylvania,	July 25, 1883.
J. S. Kountz,	Ohio,	July 24, 1884,
S. S. Burdette,	Washington, D. C.,	June 24, 1885.
L. Fairchild,	Wisconsin,	Aug. 4, 1886.
John P. Rea,	Minnesota,	Sept. 28, 1887.
William Warner,	Missouri,	Sept. 12, 1888.
Russell A. Alger,	Michigan,	Aug. 28, 1889.
W. G. Veasey,	Vermont,	Aug. 12, 1890.

Antietam.

At the battle of Antietam the slaughter was so swift and furious that the sluggish little stream, from which the battle takes its name, was discolored for many yards with human blood.

I'd woo thy solitude, sweet stream,
I'd seek thy banks at eventide;
I'd linger 'neath the sun's last beam,
And watch thy curling waters glide.

I'd hear thee sing thy gurgling song,
I'd watch thy merry ripples play;
Each leaf espy that floats along,
Or, eddy-whirled, lists on the way.

I'd strive to win thy confidence,
List to thy ceaseless murmuring strife;—
Win thy unguarded innocence,
To sing some secret of thy life.

Wouldst tell me of the fearful day,
When battling hosts with glittering arms
Crowded your banks in deadly fray,
And filled the air with war's alarms?

How, 'midst the storm of fire and hail,
The noble warior nobly fell;
How life-blood flowed—how dread his wail—
How whizzed the shot—how shrieked the shell?

How crimson-colored was thy breast,
Now splashing heedlessly along,

Now curling calmly, as at rest,
Or filling space with mournful song?

I would no more thy horrors know,
No more would hear the doleful strain
Of man's death agony: no more go
O'er battle-field 'midst scores of slain!

Flow on, then, limpid, lingering stream—
Bright waters speed thee on thy way!
Play, ripples, play, beneath the beam
Of moon by night, of sun by day.

For stainless now, thy crystal flood,
No death-cries haunt you as of yore;
Old ocean holds your tide of blood,
And drowns your death-cries in his roar.
—*T. E. Royall.*

MEMBERSHIP

OF THE

GRAND ARMY OF THE REPUBLIC.

The following was the entire reported membership of the Grand Army of the Republic for the quarter ended Sept. 30, 1890.

For the information of those who are without ready access to current statistics of the ordor, the following distribution as to States and Territories will, it is believed, be acceptable.

States.	Posts.	Members.	States.	Posts.	Members.
Alabama,	14	381	Montana,	21	794
Arizona,	10	456	Nebraska,	282	8,012
Arkansas,	66	3,749	New Hamp'e.	93	5,162
Califoania,	126	6,973	New Jersey,	119	7,843
Col. & Wyom.	84	3,272	New Mexico,	10	356
Connecticut,	92	7,241	New York,	656	39,885
Delaware,	23	1,474	North Dakota	33	859
Florida;	21	893	Ohio,	723	47,273
Georgia,	11	487	Oregon,.	49	1,784
Idaho,	23	946	Pennsylvania	607	45,273
Illinois,	621	34,315	Rhode Island,	22	2,762
Indiana,	527	27,043	South Dakota	14	407
Iowa,	436	21,382	Tennessee,	74	3,371
Kansas,	492	19,326	Texas,	34	914
Kentucky,	148	6,027	Utah,	3	168
Louisa.& Miss.	19	1,443	Vermont,	109	5,378
Maine,	161	10,851	Virginia,	39	1,416
Massachusetts	207	22,453	Wash&Alaska	54	1,994
Maryland,	45	2,326	West Vergina	95	3,017
Michigan,	407	21,817	Wisconsin,	272	14,581
Minnesota,	181	8,003			
Missouri,	428	20,326	Total,	7441	432,510

COST OF THE CIVIL WAR.

War is always a costly pastime, and the recent struggle in this country, from 1861 to 1865, was no exception. The following statement of money expended for all purposes, necessarily growing out of the civil war, with the exception of pensions, which now annually exceed $150,000,000, has been prepared with care, and will prove an interesting and instructive exhibit. It will be observed that this exhibit includes none of the *ordinary* expenses of the government:

Expenses of national loan and currency,..............$	51,522,730
Premiums,..	59,738,617
Interest on public debt,..................................	2,701,256,198
Subsistance,...	361,417,348
Quartermaster's department,............................	299,481,917
Incidental expenses of the Quartermaster's department	85,342,733
Transportation of the army,.............................	336,793,385
Transportation of officers and their baggage,...........	3,025,219
Clothing for the army,..................................	345,543,880
Purchase of horses for cavalry and artillery,............	126,672,423
Barracks, quarters, &c.,................................	31,070,846
Heating and cooking stoves,............................	448,731
Pay, milage, general expenses, etc., of army,...........	97,084,729
Pay of two and three year volunteers,..................	1,040,102,702
Pay of three month's volunteers,.......................	868,305
Pay, etc., of 100 days' volunteers,......................	14,386,778
Pay of militia and volunteers,..........................	6,126,952
Pay, etc., to officers and men, Department of Missouri.	844,150
Supplies for 100 days' volunteers,.....................	4,824,827
Bounty to volunteers and regulars on enlistment,......	38,522,046
Bounty to volunteers, other than widows and heirs....	81,760,345
Additional bounty (Act of July 28th, 1866),............	69,998,786
Collection and payment of bounty to colored soldiers,..	268,158
Reimbursing States for money expended for payment of military service to the United States,............	9,635,512
Expenses of minute men and volunteers in Ohio, Pennsylvania, Maryland, Indiana and Kentucky,.........	597,178
Expenses of recruiting,.................................	1,297,966
Draft and substitute fund,..............................	9,713,883
Medical and hospital department,.......................	45,108,770
Medical and surgical history,...........................	196,048
Providing for comfort of sick, wounded and discharged soldiers..	2,232,785
Freedmen's hospital and asylum,........................	123,487
Artificial limbs and appliances,........................	508,283
Ordnance service,.....................................	4,553,551

—14—

Ordnance and ordnance stores,	55,833,932
Armament of fortifications,	10,281,472
National armories, arsenals, etc.,	23,603,489
Purchase of arms for volunteers and regulars,	76,378,935
Expenses under Reconstruction acts,	3,128,905
Secret service,	631,587
Medals of honor	29,890
Support of National Home,	8,546,184
Publication of records of the war,	170,098
Contingencies of army and Adjutant-Genral's dept.	2,726,698
Preparing register of volunteers,	1,015
Military telegraph	2,500,085
Maintainance of gunboat fleet,	5,244,684
Keeping, transporting and supplying prisoners of war.	7,659,411
Construction of steam rams,	1,370,730
Signal service,	143,797
Gunboats on western rivers,	3,239,314
Delivering and supplying arms to loyal citizens in rebellious States,	1,649,506
Collecting, organizing and drilling volunteers,	29,091,666
Tool and siege trains,	702,250
Completing defenses of Washington,	912,283
Commutation of rations, prisoners of war in rebel States	20,636
National cemeteries,	4,162,848
Purchase of Ford's theatre,	88,000
Headstones for National cemeteries,	1,080,185
Capture of Jefferson Davis,	97,031
Support of Freedman's Bureau,	11,454,237
Claims for Quartermaster's stores and commissary sup	850,220
Claims of loyal citizens for supplies furnished,	4,170,304
Horses and other property lost in service,	4,281,724
Fertification of northern frontier,	683,748
Pay of the navy,	74,462,304
Provisions for the navy,	16,368,623
Clothing for the navy,	1,594,790
Construction and repairs,	134,178,096
Equipment of vessels,	25,174,614
Ordnance,	31,422,094
Surgeon's supplies,	1,937,744
Yards and docks,	30,300,302
Fuel for the navy,	11,340,332
Hemp for the navy,	898,252
Steam machinery,	40,297,318

Navigation,	2,526,247
Navy hospital,	499,662
Magazines,	404,531
Marine Corps (pay, clothing, etc)	7,757,615
Naval academy,	1,862,132
Temporary increase of navy,	8,123,766
Miscellaneous expenses,	2,614,044
Bounties to seamen,	2,821,550
Bounties for destroying vessels,	271,309
Indemnity for losses,	289,025
Grand total, exclusive of pensions,	$6,775,929,908

SOME INTERESTING FACTS.

The following interesting facts as to the history of the war for the Union have been compiled from reliable sources, and, it is believed, will prove both entertaining and valuable:

In all there were 1,882 engagements.

There were 2,011 regiments in the Union armies.

The three days' Union loss at Gettysburg was 25,218.

The first 38 New York regiments were enlisted for two year.

There were twenty-five infantry corps in the Union armies.

**

The State of New York furnished to the army 467,047 enlisted men.

**

There were 45 regiments of infantry that lost over 200 men killed during the war.

**

The cavalry corps of the Armies of the East and the West lost 10,596 killed in action.

**

There were 112 battles in the war, in which one side or the other lost over 500 killed and wounded.

**

In the civil war the Union armies lost 110,070 killed in action; 275,175 wounded; 199,720 died of disease; besides all those "missing in action."

**

On Sept. 30, 1890, there were 561,938 pensioners of all classes borne upon the rolls of the Washington office; and the annual disbursement for pensions during the ensuing year will exceed $155,000,000.

**

Antietam was the bloodiest battle of the war begun and concluded in a single day. The fighting began at sunrise and ended at 4 o'clock, with a total loss on the Union side of 12,410 killed, wounded and missing.

TO THE VOLUNTEERS OF OTSEGO CO.

MORE than 30 years ago the struggle for the existence of the nation had fairly opened, eleven states had seceded, a separate government had been organized, the confederates had committed the first act of war by firing upon the flag at Fort Sumter, when the lightning had flashed the telegram to the loyal people of the north that Sumter was in possession of the Southern Confederacy and Major Anderson and his gallant band had surrendered as prisoners of war. There were, within the boundaries of Otsego county, many who had hoped for peace; but now all knew and recognized that, if the Union was preserved at all, it could only be done by force of arms, and the patriotic sons of Otsego county were rallying to the support of their imperiled country. On the 15th day of April, 1861, the President of the United States issued his first call for 75,000 volunteers. In less than 48 hours from the promulgation of that call, the ranks were filled; and, not only were these in column, but behind this 75,000, stood more than two and one-half millions who, in the light of subsequent history, were ready to go down to battle. In this first contingent, Otsego county had nearly 400 men, and from the commencement of the contest to its termination, under all the calls for troops, this county supplied more than 6,500 volunteers to all branches of the service. Of this little army, which manifested such self-sacrificing devotion, a little less than 2,500 remain residents of the county from which they took up arms, and more than half that number lie buried where they fell, facing the foe. Wherever duty called, whether in camp or hospital, on battle field or in prison, on the weary march or in the protracted siege, they ever exhibited sublime loyalty and undaunted courage. Never did the flag go down on battle field or bloody death, on land or sea, but their hands were there to lift it up. They stood on the lonely picket watches of the war, in the trenches, on the dead line, on the long march with Sherman from Atlanta to the Sea, wherever the tide of battle ebbed and flowed, in the east and in the west, on the bloody fields of Virginia and Georgia, at Bull Run, Cold Harbor or on the Peninsula, at Antietam, at Port Hudson, at Petersburg, at Chancellorville and in the crowning victory at Gettysburg; where the wave of Rebel invasion was forever dashed back, as it beat in vain against the solid lines of Cemetery Hill, at Wilson's creek, at Malvern Hill or fought under "Old Joe Hooker" above the clouds; and, from the crimson crest of Lookout Mountain, looked down on their former lives as little in comparison with one great deed. Where the Rebel fire was hottest and the bullets the thickest could be found the brave soldiers of Otsego county facing the foe and fighting with unflinching devotion and loftiest courage for their Country's flag. Read the story of how they suffered, how they fought and how they died in every bloody battle field from Bull Run, Appomatox, at Antietam, Cold Horbor, in the last desperate charge on the bloody field of Chancellorville. Read it at Gettysburg or on the frozen banks of Stone River. These are the imperishable records of the gallant sons of Otsego. They are of the Nation's heros! They were the defenders of its honor! They are of the men who saved its life!

The Old Man and Jim.

Old man never had much to say—
   'Ceptin' to Jim,—
An Jim was the wildest boy he had—
   And the Old man jes' wrapped up in him!
Never heard him speak but once
Er twice in my life;—and first time was
When the army broke out, and Jim he went,
The Old man backin' him fer three months,—
And all 'at I heard the Old man say
Was, jes' as he turned to start away,—
   "Well; good-bye Jim:
        Take keer of yourse'f!"

'Peard like, he was more satisfied
   'Jes' *lookin'* at Jim
And likin' him all to hisse'f like, see,—
   'Cause he was jes' wrapped up in him!
And over and over I mind the day
The Old man come and stood round in the way
While we was drillin', a watchin' Jim—
And down at the depot a-heerin' him say,—
   "Well; good-bye, Jim:
        Take keer of yourse'f!"

Never was nothin' about the farm
   Disting'ished Jim;—
Neighbors all ust to wonder why
   The Old man 'peared wrapped up in him;
But when Cap. Biggler, he rit back
'At Jim was the bravest boy he had
In the whole dern rigiment, white er black,
And his fightin' good as his farmin' bad--
   'At he had led, with a bullet clean
Bored through his thigh, and carried the flag
Through the bloodiest battle you ever seen,—
The old man wound up a letter to him

'At Cap. read to us, 'at said, — "Tell Jim
  Good-bye:
                And take keer of hisse'f."

Jim come back jes' long enough
  To take the whim
'At he like to go back in the cavalry—
  And the Old man jes' wrapped up in him!—
Jim 'lowed 'at he'd had sich luck afore,
Guessed he'd tackle her three years more.
And the Old man gave him a colt he'd raised
And follored him over to Camp Ben Wade,
And laid around fer a week er so
Watchin' Jim on dress parade—
Tel finally he rid away,
And last he heerd was the Old man say,—
  "Well; good-bye, Jim:
            Take keer of yourse'f!"

Tuk the papers, the Old man did,
  A-watchin' fer Jim—
Fully believin' he'd make his mark
  Some way—jes' wrapped up in him!—
And many a time the word 'u'd come
'At stirred him up like the tap of a drum—
At Petersburg, fer instance, where
Jim rid right into their cannons there,
And tuk 'em, and p'inted 'em t'other way,
And socked it home to the boys in gray,
As they skooted for timber, and on and on—
Jim a lieutenant and one arm gone,
And the Old man's words in his mind all day,—
  "Well; good-bye, Jim:
            Take keer of yourse'f!"

Think of a private now, perhaps,
  We'll say like Jim,
'At's clumb clean up to the shoulder-straps—
  And the Old man jes' wrapped up in him!
Think of him—with the war plum' through,
And the glorious old Red-White-and Blue
A-laughin' the news down over Jim
And the Old man, bendin' over him—
The surgeon turnin' away with tears

'At hadn't leaked fer years and years—
As the hand of the dyin' boy clung to
His father's, the old voice in his ears,—
 "Well, good-bye, Jim;
   Take keer of yourse'f!"
                    —*James Whitcomb Riley.*

SUMMARY OF LOSSES FROM WAR IN TWENTY-FIVE YEARS.

KILLED IN BATTLE OR DIED OF WOUNDS AND DISEASE.

Crimean war,	750,000
Italian war, 1859,	45,000
War of Schleswig Holstein,	3,000
American Civil War—North,	309,000
American Civil War—South,	520,000
War between Prussia, Austria and Italy, 1886,	45,000
Expeditions to Mexico, Cochin China, Morocco, Paraguay, &c.,	65,000
Franco-German War, 1870—1870, France,	155,000
Franco-German War, 1870—1871, Germany,	50,000
Russian and Turkish War of 1877,	225,000
Zulu and Afghan Wars of 1879,	40,000
Total,	2,188,000

STATEMENT.

Of the number of men furnished (exclusive of the navy) by each State, Territory and District of Columbia, from April 15th, 1861, to the close of the war:

States & Territories.	Total.	States & Territories.	Total.
Maine,	72,114	Kansas,	20,151
New Hampshire	34,629	Tennessee,	31,092
Vermont,	35,262	Arkansas,	8,289
Massachusetts,	152,048	North Carolina,	3,156
Rhode Island,	23,609	California,	15,725
Connecticut	57,379	Nevada,	1,080
New York,	467,047	Oregon,	1,810
New Jersey,	81,010	Washington Ter.,	964
Pennsylvania,	366,107	Nebraska Territory,	3,157
Delaware,	13,670	Colorado Territory,	4,903
Maryland,	50,316	Dakota Territory,	206
West Virginia,	32,068	New Mexico Ter.,	6,561
Dist. of Columbia,	16,872	Alabama,	2,576
Ohio,	319,659	Florida,	1,290
Indiana,	197,147	Louisiana,	5,224
Illinois,	259,147	Mississippi,	545
Michigan,	89,372	Texas,	1,965
Wisconsin,	96,424	Indian Nation,	3,530
Minnesota,	25,052	Colored Troops,	99,337
Iowa,	76,309		
Missouri,	109,111	Total,	2,865,028
Kentucky,	79,025		

ARMY STATISTICS.

In the war of the Revolution, 1775 to 1783, the troops enlisted from the original thirteen states, were: 1775, total 37,363; 1776, 89,761; 1777, 63,720; 1778, 51,049; 1779, 43,076; 1781, 29,340; 1782, 18,006 and in 1783, 13,477; total 350,789.

.

In the war with Great Britain, 1812 to 1815. Total, July, 1812, 6,686; February, 1813, 19,039; September, 1814, 68,186; February, 1815, 33,424. The whole militia force raised during the war was 31,210 officers and 440,412 men, the total being 471,632.

.

The war with Mexico, 1846 to 1848. Whole number of troops in the Regular Army, including marines, was: 17,506; whole number of volunteers, 73,776; total 101,282. Of these 1,049 were killed in battle; 508 died of wounds; 8,420 were wounded.

.

The grand total of United States troops in the late Civil war, was; 2,865,028, of which, 99,337, were colored troops. The Provost Marshal General reported the number killed in battle as commissioned officers 5,221; enlisted men 62,-580; died of wounds, commissioned officers 3,221; enlisted men 34,727; died of disease 199,720; total deaths 289,036; desertions 199,105.

.

A partial or estimated statement of soldiers in the Confederate service who died of wounds or disease is given at 133,821; desertions, 104,428. The number of United States troops taken prisoners during the Civil war was 212,608; number Confederate troops 476,169; number of United States troops paroled on the field 16,431; of Confederate troops 248,599. Number of United States troops who died while prisoners 29,725; of Confederate troops 26,774. Grand total of soldiers furnished in these four wars were 2,782,825.

THE ARMY DURING THE CIVIL WAR.

The following table shows the dates of the President's proclamation for men, the number of men called for and the number secured:

Date of President's Proclamation.	Number Called for	Period of Service.	Number Obtained.
April 15, 1861,	75,000	3 months	93,326
May 3, 1861	82,748	3 years	714,221
July 22 and 25, 1861.	500,000		
May and June, 1862.	500,000	3 months	15,007
July 2, 1862.	300,000	3 years	431,958
August 4, 1862.	300,000	9 months	87,588
June 15, 1863.	100,000	6 months	16,361
October 17, 1863.	300,000	2 years	374,807
February 1, 1864.	200,000		
March 14, 1864.	200,000	3 years	284,021
April 23, 1864.	85,000	100 days	83,652
July 18, 1864.	500,000	1,2,3 years	384,882
December 19, 1864.	300,000	1,2,3 years	204,568
Total,	2,942,748		2,690,401

STRENGTH OF THE FEDERAL ARMY.

DATE.	On Duty.	Absent.	Total.
January 1, 1861,	14,663	1,704	16,367
July 1, 1861,	183,588	3,163	186,751
January 1, 1862,	527,204	48,714	575,917
January 1, 1863,	698,800	219,389	918,081
January 1, 1864,	611,250	249,487	860,737
January 1, 1865,	620,924	338,536	959,460
May 1, 1865,	797,807	202,709	1,000,516

THE BIVOUAC OF THE DEAD.

There were killed in action, or died of wounds, in the Civil war—commissioned officers 5,221; enlisted men 104,849. Died from disease or accident—commissioned officers 2,321; enlisted men 197,399, making a total loss of 309,790, besides all those missing in action. Deaths which occurred after the men left the army are not included in these figures.

WAR.

The cost of recent wars, according to figures furnished by the London Peace Society, is as follows:

Crimean war,	£ 340,000,000
Italian war, 1859,	460,000,000
American Civil War—North,	60,000,000
American Civil War—South,	940,000,000
Schleswig Holstein war,	7,000,000
Austrian and Prussia, 1866,	66,000,000
Expeditions to Mexico, Morocco, &c.,	40,000,000
Franco-Prussian war,	500,000,000
Russian and Turkish war, 1877,	210,000,000
Zulu and Afghan wars, 1879,	30,000,000
Total,	£ 2,653,000,000

This would allow $10.00 for every man, woman and child on the habitable globe. It would make two railways all around the world at $250,000 per mile each.

Hall Post, No. 139,

LAURENS, N. Y.

Regular meeting every Thursday at G. A. R. Hall.

THIS Post was organized and charter received July 11, 1890, and mustered into the department of New York July 19, 1890, at Richmond Hall, Laurens, by mustering officer James Roberts, of E. D. Farmer Post. No. 119, of Oneonta, N. Y.

The Post was named for James and LeRoy Hall, two honored and respected sons of Laurens. They were brave soldiers, enlisting in the 121st N. Y. V., Co. I., James as private and LeRoy as drummer. The record of this Regiment at Fredricksburg, Rappahannock Station at Gettysburg, Salem Heights, Spotsylvania, Cold Harbor, Fisher Hill, Petersburg and Cedar Creek, will never be forgotten. Many gallant comrades have gloriously fallen in the storm of battle while bravely defending their country in many hard fought battles with the 121st N. Y. Volunteers.

James Hall was a brave soldier, a true friend of a genial disposition and a social companion, serving with his regiment, participating in all its battles and marches until the winter of 1862, when he was stricken with fever and died at Bell Plain, Va., Dec. 23, 1862. LeRoy remained with his regiment, participating in its battles and sharing its hardships until the close of the war. When you

PLEASE REMEMBER!

W. C. STRONG,
)THE(—

Laurens Tailor,

Makes Pants to Order, $3 to $9,
Suits that Fit,   - $15 to $35,

UNIFORMS AND HATS
For G. A. R. Posts
AT SPECIAL PRICES.

Trunks, Bags, Hats and Caps.

LARGE LINE OF

Overalls, Underwear, Gloves, Etc.

All the Latest Magazines and Story Papers.
New Novels, Etc., on our News Stand.

D. S. PEET,
—)DEALER IN(—

Hardware and Drugs

And Wholesale Butter Buyer,

LAURENS,   -   -   N. Y.

read the record of the 121st Regiment you have read his record. Always at his post, full of life and vigor, looking only to the bright side of life, making those happy around him. He was discharged and mustered out of service June 25, 1865. Took up his residence in Oneonta, where he was killed by accident.

Their graves each Memorial Day bears a profusion of flowers placed there by Comrades of the G. A. R. Post and loving friends and neighbors. Mrs. LeRoy Hall is now residing at Oneonta, N. Y., and the widowed mother is residing at Laurens, N. Y. Through them and their efforts the Hall Post were recently presented with a handsome picture of each of the two heroes.

The first Commander elected was James N. Vosburgh, born at Charlestown, (then Schoharie) Montgomery Co., N. Y., April 26, 1836. When one year old went with his parents to Barnes Hollow, and at the age of 7 years moved to Oneida Co., where he completed his education. Leaving school in 1846 went to work in Cotton Mills as an operator. When 18 years old went to Springfield Center to learn a trade (that of a machinest) with Shipman & Son. Removing to Fort Plain and then to Clark Mills, Oneida Co., where he completed his trade, where he remained until 1862, when he enlisted as private, Aug. 7th, 1862, in Co. D, 117, N. Y. V., at Rome, N. Y., and mustered in at Camp Huntington, August 20, 1862, under Capt. John M. Wolcott. Ordered to Washington and thence to Turley Town, five miles from Washington, when the regiment was broken up and the companys sent in different directions. Co. B was sent to Battery, Vermont; remained here until October, when they were sent to Fort Ripley, where they were to re-join the regiment. Remained here until Dec. 23; crossed the river to Fort Baker the 16th of April and landed at Norfolk, Virginia: thence to Suffolk, to Calhoon Point down to Julian Creek,

THE CRANDALL Type Writer.

A MODEL OF ECONOMY, UTILITY AND DURABILITY,

At $50.00.

This is a strictly first-class two handed TYPE WRITER, inferior to none in utility, range of work, speed and convenience, and has the following points to distinguish it from others:

1. — Work always in sight.
2. — Instantly changable Type; 8 styles in English.
3. — Letters cannot get out of "alignment."
4. — One-half the price usually paid for any article that will do anything like the same work.

If you think of purchasing a Machine, don't invest your **One Hundred Dollars** until you make a trial of the CRANDALL, and if you haven't thought of buying one before, the low price is worth serious thought.

We will send the CRANDALL to responsible parties on one week's trial, giving them an opportunity to demonstrate the correctness of our claim, that this Type Writer is equal in all respects and superior to Machines that are sold at $100.

Factory at Groton, N. Y.

NEW YORK OFFICE, 353 BROADWAY.   CHICAGO OFFICE, 237 LASELLE ST.

Send for Catalogue.

Crandall Machine Company,
GROTON,   -   N. Y.

building breast works. In June went to Yorktown, thence to White House landing, where the army was reorganized. Then was sent up the Peninsula to King Williams Court House to Hanover Junction. July 4th went back to Yorktown, returning to camp near Portsmouth July 14. Ordered to Folly Island July 28, 1863. Sick with fever at Balfour Hospital, Portsmouth. Joined regiment at Folly Island Sept. 1863. Shortly after was sent to Beaufort, S. C., to hospital. Joined regiment Dec. 10 and remained till April 9. Ordered with regiment to Glouchester, Va.; thence to West Point, up the James to Bermuda Hundred, participating in many battles. Dec. 1864, went to Fort Fisher under the disastrous raid of Gen. Butler, and Jan. 5, under Gen. Terry, made the second attempt to capture Fort Fisher, landing the 14, capturing the Fort the 15. Was wounded in this battle and sent to McDougal Hospital at Fort Scuyler, N. Y. Harbor. Discharged April 3, 1865 and returned to Oneida Co.

Joined Rowell Post at Waterville, N. Y., Oct. 8, 1869. Joined by card Pettit Post 86, of Clayville, and elected Commander to serve during 1877. This Post disbanding, organized the Joe Boney Post at Chenango July, 12, 1878, and elected first Commander. 1884 joined by card Ross Post 31 N. Y. Mills. Was discharged from this Post and organized Hall Post, 139, at Laurens. At the first meeting July 19, 1890, was elected Commander for ballance the of the year through wise management and thorough disciplin the Post soon became one of prominence in the department and he was elected in Dec. to succeed himself.

J. F. Newell, present Commander, was born at Milford, N. Y., Nov. 25, 1840. Educated at the common schools in that place. Moved to Hartwick in 1860, embarking into the jewelery business, from which place he enlisted Oct. 18, 1861, as a recruit for 39th regiment N. Y. V. Was mus-

DAULEY & WRIGHT

Marble and Granite Works,

43 & 45 Broad Street,
ONEONTA, N. Y.

We shall be pleased to hear from parties considering the erection of any kind of cemetery improvements, and will be pleased to submit designs estimates, etc., for consideration and inspection, or to furnish any information, whether the purchase of work has been decided upon or not. If a design has already been adopted, an estimate will be promptly given. Special designs will be furnished parties contemplating work of this character. Parties ordering may rest assured of obtaining first-class stock, superior workmanship, and the lowest possible prices consistent with good work. We have always a fine line of new and original designs. The latest styles. Work delivered to any place in the state in first-class condition.

tered in at Cherry Valley and ordered to Albany, joining the 76th Reg. N. Y. V. under Captain A. L. Swan. Was ordered to front at Washington; remaining until spring of 1862, when they were ordered to Fredricksburg. The 18th of June was taken with fever and sent to Carver hospital, Washington. Remaining here a short time when he was sent to David Island, remaining two months. Was then granted a short furlough to visit his home at Milford. Not being able to return to his regiment at the expiration of furlogh granted, it was extended and he remained at Milford until the following spring, when he rejoined his regiment at Pratt's Point, Va., participating in the battle of Gettysburg. Afterwards was transferred to the Reserve Corps, stationed at Washington during the winter, doing guard duty. From here they were sent to Lafayette, Ind., to enforce the draft. Was discharged Oct. 26, 1864 and returned to Milford, soon after going to Cooperstown, working at his trade as jeweler until 1866, when he went to Oneonta, and was charter member of E. D. Farmer Post, Oneonta, N. Y. In 1871 he went to Milford and engaged in the furniture business and removed to Laurens in 1873. Took card from Farmer Post and is a charter member of Hall Post 139. Was elected adjutant and later Commander to serve during 1892.

Held the office of Town Clerk eight years, Justice of the Peace eleven years, which office he holds at the present time. Was Post Master under Arthur's administration and re-appointed under Harrison's.

W. L. Hopkins, born at Laurens Oct. 27, 1844; attending school at Canandiagua academy, completing his education at Hartwick Seminary. After leaving school enlisted in Co. H, 152d Regiment; mustered in at Herkimer, N. Y., Sept. 25, 1862, as 2d Lieutenant. Ordered to Washington at Chain Bridge camp for the winter, and in the spring was ordered back to Carrol Hill, near Washington.

IRON CHIMNEY CAPS!

J. MAYNE, * * *

Iron * Founder,

If you want your chimneys to last cover them, as it is impossible to keep a chimney in order without some kind of protection. Our new Iron Cap is the best and cheapest, besides being very ornamental. They are easily applied by anyone and will preserve a chimney a life-time, provided the chimney is in good condition when the cap is used. They are sold plain or with cresting, and the price is so low that people cannot afford to do without them. We can give first-class references from parties who have them in use, having sold over 500 in Oneonta and vicinity alone. Six sizes. Send for price list. Agents wanted.

J. MAYNE,

ONEONTA, - - N. Y.

In January was sent to Arlington Heights before medical director and discharged upon surgeon's certificate for general disability Jan. 14, 1863; returned to Laurens and began farming. Is now a charter member of Hall Post. 139; a prominent Mason, member of Lodge 548, F. & A. M., Laurens, N. Y.

H. B. Dummer was born at Auburn, N. Y., Jan. 17, 1833. When 7 years old his mother died and he went on a farm, remaining two years; removed to Niagara Co., town of Cambria, soon after going to Waterford, Saratoga Co., and learned the tinsmith trade, where he remained until 21 years old. Enlisted at Watertown, N. Y., in Co. H, 115th N. Y. Vol., Aug. 5, 1862. Mustered in at Camp Fonda, going direct to Baltimore, arriving at the monumental city Aug. 31. Sept. 13 engaged in battle at Maryland Heights, Sept. 14, battle of Harper Ferry, the 115 holding the extreme right. Sept. 15, after two day's fighting, the rebels demanded the surrender of Harper Ferry and the Union Army, Gen. Miles complying with the demand without hesitation. The Union troops were paroled and sent to Chicago to Camp Douglas, the 115th occupying the stalls in the Iowa State fair grounds. Remained here two months and returned to Washington Dec. 28. At Fortress Monroe received orders to report to Gen. Keys at Yorktown, Jan. 23 sailed from Fortress Monroe, arriving there Col. reported to Gen. Dix and received sealed orders to report to Gen. Hunter at Hilton Head, S. C., and were placed under the guns of Fort Hunter. While on dress parade orders were read. The Regiment had been court marshaled and sentenced to one year without pay for burning the barracks at Camp Douglass, an accusation which was withdrawn and ammends made by the Government soon after Col. Simmons had visited Washington and placed the facts before the War Department, the barracks having been burned by other soldiers

Established  1877.

OFFICE OF

ASA G. STRONG,

No. 19 Deitz St., -:- ONEONTA, N. Y.

General Agent for the

White ~ Sewing ~ Machine.

Awarded First Prize at the Cincinnati exposition in 1888, and at the World's Fair at Paris in 1889, for being the

Best Family Sewing Machine.

ALSO sell all other kinds of Sewing Machines, Needles, Attachments and Parts for all kinds of Sewing Machines. Do not be deceived by agents selling only one kind of machine, on commission, claiming that to be the best, as it is the only kind they have, they must sell you that or nothing. I buy my machines direct from the manufacturers for CASH and can give you your choice of any kind manufactured and on the most favorable terms.

OIL for sale at wholesale and retail, - - - -
- - - *All Kinds of Sewing Machine Repairs.*

WRITE AND TELL ME WHAT YOU WANT

ASA G. STRONG,

Oneonta, .:. New York.

while moving stoves after the 115th had left. From Hilton Head went to Beaufort, S. C., remaining until fall, doing garrison duty; thence to Florida, engaging in the battle of Oluskee Feb. 20, where the Regiment was terribly cut up; thence up St. John's river. Fell back to Hilton Head; thence to Bermuda Hundreds, Va. Engaged in the battles of Pilatk's March 16, Bermuda Hundreds May 5 and Chesterfield Heights, Va., May 7, 1864, and thence to White House and fought battle at New Cold Harbor; fell back to City Point and skermish at Petersburg until the first attack at Fort Fisher Dec. 1864. Assault and capture of Fort Fisher Jan. 15, 1865. Was wounded at the battle of Oulstee Feb. 20, 1864. Discharged at Rolly June 17, 1865 and returned to Waterford, remaining two weeks. In 1876 went to Troy and from there to Connecticut in 1880, and in 1888 moved to Laurens. Charter member of Hall Post and upon its organization was elected Quartermaster and is at present filling the same office.

John Thornton, born at Machias, Cattaragus Co., Sept. 9, 1833, where he was educated. In 1850 moved to Crawford Co., Pa., and in 1855 to Coventry, Chenango County, where he had charge of a saw mill. Enlisted in 1861 as private in a company recruited for Light Artillery, attached to McClellan's rifles, going to Park Row barracks, N. Y., where they remained for two weeks. There existed some dissatisfaction in the company when they found that they could not join the McClellan rifles, so they were ordered to Ricker Island from here, where they remained four weeks; thence to Staten Island and ordered to New York. While here he was sent back to recruit a company. Procuring a number of recruits turned them over to Capt. Lock, who was then organizing a company at Binghamton, and in the fall of 1862, enlisted as private in Co. H,

76th N. Y. V., as private. Ordered to Washington and to the front, participating in the battles of Culpeper, Arlington Heights and second Bull Run. Sent to Emery hospital where he remained until spring, rejoining regiment at the Wilderness. In April, having but 35 men left, they were consolidated with the 147th. Was wounded and sent to Appomattox Court House, headquarters of Gen. Lee. Took boat for New York and afterwards sent to Elmira to care for wounded men. Discharged at Elmira June, 1865. Moved to Portlandville in 1867 and to Laurens in 1878. Joined C. C. Siver Post. Is charter member of Hall Post. Junior Vice for first six months after its organization. Was Senior Vice Commander for 1891 and is at present Quarter Master Sargeant. He is a prominent member of Odd Fellows lodge and Good Templar.

Jeremiah B. Strait enlisted as privat in Co. H, 152, N. Y. Vol., Aug. 28, 1862. In the fall of 1863 was sent to Army Square hospital, Washington. April 18, 1864 was transferred to the invalid corps and discharged for general disability Sept. 3, 1864.

ALL THE SOLDIERS BUY

Pianos, Organs, Musical Merchandise, Sheet Music and Books

OF

Fisher & Ogden,

No. 174 Main St., ONEONTA, N.Y.

Because they are a reliable firm and sell honest goods at an honest price.

A trial will Certainly Convince any.

OFFICERS OF HALL POST.

J. F. Newell, ... Commander.
J. B. Straight, ... Senior Vice-Commander.
Samuel A. Clark, ... Junior Vice-Commander.
Henry VanBuren, ... Chaplain.
W. C. Saelsbury, ... Surgeon.
James N. Vosburgh, ... Officer of the Day.
Edson Wright, ... Officer of the Grand.
Henry B. Dummer, ... Quartermaster.
Rush Strain, ... Adjutant.
Hiram Persons, ... Sergeant Major.
John Thornton, ... Quartermaster Sergeant.

PAST COMMANDER,—James N. Vosburgh.

LIST OF MEMBERS.

Adsit, James A., ... I 144 N. Y.
Brigg, Lewis C., ... H 152 N. Y.
Baily, Alvin, ... G 5 N. Y. Art.
Carr, Hiram .... I 152 N. Y.
Clark, Samuel A., ... D 22 N. Y. Cav.
Dummer, Henry B., ... H 115 N. Y.
Eldred, Jerome B., ... H 30 Wis.
Edson, Henry .... Unknown.
Hopkins, W. L., ... F 152 N. Y.
Hay, Walter S., ... B 4 heavy Art.
Joslin, Edward, ... K 43 N. Y.
Newell, J. F., ... H 76 N. Y.
Pickens, Alvin, ... I 76 N. Y.
Persons, Hiram, ... G 110 N. Y.
Ramsey, Stephen, ... Unknown.
Sperry, Henry J., ... I 20 N. Y. Cav.
Strain, Rush, ... G 95 N. Y.
Saelsbury, W. C., ... H 76 N. Y.
Straight, J. B., ... H 152 N. Y.
Tilley, Cortland, ... G. 3 N. Y. Cav.

GILBERT W. GOLDSMITH, D. D. S.,

OPERATIVE DENTIST.

CROWN AND BRIDGE WORK
OR
TEETH WITHOUT PLATES
A SPECIALTY.

➤ Eleven Years Practice in the Great City of New York. ≼

FORD BLOCK, OPPOSITE CENTRAL HOTEL,

ONEONTA, - - New York.

C. F. MAYHAM,

ATTORNEY AND COUNSELOR AT LAW

AND

PENSION AND GOVERNMENT CLAIM ATTORNEY,

OFFICE FORD BLOCK,

ONEONTA, - N. Y.

➤ A. ✢ R. ✢ SMITH, ≼

MANUFACTURER OF

ALL ✱ KINDS ✱ OF ✱ HARNESS

AND DEALER IN

BLANKETS, ROBES, WHIPS, BRUSHES,

AND ALL KINDS OF HORSE FURNISHINGS.

CORNER MAIN AND BROAD STREETS,
Under Ford's Jewelery Store,

Oneonta, - - New York.

Tinney, Silas, ...G 1 N. Y.
Thornton, John, ...H 76 N. Y.
Voorhies, Edgar H., ...I 152 N. Y.
Vosburgh, James N., ...D 117 N. Y.
VanBuren, Henry, ...F 137 N. Y.
Whitmarsh, Hiram, ...H 152 N. Y.
Weldon, Leroy, ...G 19 N. Y.
Wellman, Henry Z., ...F 137 N. Y.
Wright, Edson, ...G 141 N. Y.

OUR VALIANT BRAVES.

BY WESLIE P. MORSE.

Give honor to the valiant braves,
The blue survivors of the fray,
Who faced death at our country's call,
And made us what we are to-day.
Those noble men who fought and bled;
Yea, bravely offered up their lives,
And suffered untold misery
During the dreadful, civil strife.

'Tis true, we never can repay
the debt of gratitude we owe.
To make life pleasant for them now,
Our hearts should ever glow;
Ever to treat them with respect;
Extend a cordial, friendly hand.
By them the Union was preserved;
They saved our cherished, honored land.

W. H. IVES,

Jeweler

—AND—

Optician,

174 Main St.,

Oneonta, - N. Y.

You make no mistake in coming to us to select

Diamonds, Silverware, Watches, Clocks and Jewelry.

We keep a large and well selected stock of

A FINE QUALITY.

NO : SHABBY : GOODS.

We can surely please you in every respect.

W. H. IVES,
Jeweler and Optician,

174 MAIN STRRET,

Oneonta, - New York.

Col. Olcott Post, No. 522,

PORTLANDVILLE, N. Y.

Regular meetings first and third Friday of each month at G. A. R. Hall.

OLCOTT Post was organized in October, 1884, its charter received and mustered into the department of New York Oct. 30, 1884, by mustering officer, James C. Roberts, of E. D. Farmer Post, Oneonta, N. Y., assisted by eighteen delegates from that post.

The Post was named in honor of and to perpetuate the name of one of the bravest soldiers enlisting from Otsego county, Egbert Olcott. He enlisted as private in Co. C, 44th Reg., N. Y. V., and for distinguished service on the field was promoted to First Lieutenant, Captain, Major, and discharged from service as Colonel.

The first Commander was Robert M. Rose, born at Milford, N. Y., Jan. 1, 1843. Educated at Hartwick academy. Enlisted as a recruit for Co. G, 1st N. Y. Eng., joining his regiment at Hilton Head, S. C., serving with his regiment until they were discharged in July, 1865, when he returned to Milford and engaged in the hop business and farming. The Post, under his administration, soon became one of influence in the department, and he was again elected Commander to serve during the years 1887 and 1888. He was Supervisor of the town of Milford in 1875 and 1876. Member of the Chapter and of the Mt. Vision Encampment of Odd Fellows at Cooperstown, N.Y.

C. FISK,
Livery and Exchange Stables,
Barns in the Rear of the Otego House.

Fiast-Class Rigs at Reasonable Prices.
Day or Night.

MAIN ST., - OTEGO, N. Y.

➤ONEONTA➤

GOLD AND SILVER PLATING WORKS.

Work Guaranteed.  Prices Reasonable.

——) DEALER IN (——

WATCHES, CLOCKS AND JEWELRY.

GEORGE H. CHANDLER,

36 Dietz St., - ONEONTA, N. Y.

He is residing at Portlandville, his family consisting
of wife and two sons, George L., aged 24, now residing
and engaged in the hop business in Washington Territory.
Roy C., aged 18, is completing his education at Hamilton
college.

George D. Bartlett, present Commander, was elected to
succeed Mr. Rose, who had served from October, 1884 to
January, 1885. He was born at Sidney, Delaware county.
N. Y., Feb. 1847. Attended the common schools and accepted a position as clerk at Unadilla, N. Y. Enlisted
August, 1864, as a private in Co. K, 1st N. Y. Eng., as a
recruit. Joined his regiment at Morris Island. Was discharged July 4, 1865, and returned to Unadilla and completed his education at Bryant & Stratton's college at
Poughkeepsie, N. Y. Went to Virginia and from there
to Kansas and Nebraska. In 1872 returned to Portlandville. Was in the harness business eight years. In 1883
accepted a position as clerk with W. L. Wellman, dealer
in general merchandise, where he is at present employed.
Is a charter member of Post and for three years Adjutant.
That his administration of the Post affairs was appreciated by its members is shown from the fact of his being
elected Commander again to serve during 1889, and reelected each year since that time. He is a member of
Laurens Lodge, 548, F. & A. M. Is residing with his
family, wife, son and daughter, at Portlandville, N. Y.

Daniel E. Packer, born at Edmeston, Otsego county,
Oct., 1837. When four years old, with his parents, moved to Portlandville and attended the common schools and
working on a farm until 19 years old, when he learned
the blacksmith trade. Aug. 11, 1862, he enlisted as a private in Co. E, 121st N. Y. V. Mustered at Mohawk and
ordered to Fort Lincoln and through Maryland to Antiet-

Ceperley & Gardner's Steam Laundry,

ONEONTA, N. Y.

BEST IN THE COUNTY.
Try it.

ONEONTA
CLEANING + AND + DYE + WORKS,

F. J. BOURGARDE, Proprietor,

62 MAIN STREET, - - ONEONTA, N. Y.

Wet or Dry Cleaning, Repairing and Pressing neatly done Ladies' and Gentleman's Clothing Cleaned, Dyed and finished in the latest shades of colors.
Goods Delivered where ordered.

Oneonta Variety Works,

All kinds of repairing neatly and promptly done.
RAZORS AND SHEARS GROUND, GUNS, REVOLVERS, UMBRELLAS AND PARASOLS REPAIRED.

BICYCLE :-: REPAIRING
A SPECIALTY.

E. MELICK, Prop.

am. Ordered after battle to Bakersville and remained two months. Taken sick was sent to the hospital, was granted a furlough and came north. Reported to hospital at Albany in March, 1865, and by reason of general disability, was discharged and returned to Portlandville. Is a charter member and was the organizer of the Olcott Post. Has been Quartermaster since its organization. Was ordained as a minister in the Methodist church as local deacon in 1883, joining the Christian Conference in 1887 in the fall of the same year took the full ordination as an ordained elder at Delhi, Delaware county, N. Y., and is now residing at Springfield Centre.

George W. Rose, born at Milford, July 10, 1847. Educated at Hartwick Seminary. Enlisted as private in Co. D. 193 N. Y. V., at Auburn, N. Y. Ordered to Summit Point, Va., thence to Cumberland City, Md., where they were sent in detachments to different points, doing patrol duty. Rejoining regiment returned to Winchester to Woodstock for winter quarters. Discharged Jan. 18, 1866, at Harper's Ferry. Joined Olcott Post as chrrter member.

POST OFFICERS.

George D. Bartlett,.........Commander.
R. L. Garlick,................Senion Vice-Commander.
W. A. Tarbox,...............Junior Vice-Commander.
John Vandeusen,............Adjutant
D. E. Packer,..................Quartermaster.
Lewis Crawford,.............Surgeon.
Ralph Weidman,............Chaplain.
Dustin Whitney,............Officer of the Day.
Emery Potter,................Officer of the Grand.
Lewis Hopkins, ...Sergeant Major.
D. G. Winser,................Quartermaster Sergeant.

THE SINGER MANUFACTURING COMPANY'S
VIBRATING SHUTTLE NO. 2 MACHINE.

LATEST AND BEST OF ITS CLASS.

Our new design of Vibrating Shuttle Machine is the latest development of that popular principle, containing special patented improvements, which make it:

1st—The Lightest Running machine in the market.
2d—The simplest machine in the World. It requires absolutely no Teaching.
3d—The only Vibrator which makes a perfect stitch—a result heretofore attained in family machines only by our Oscillator.
4th—The only Vibrator which can sew from lightest to heaviest cotton without change of tention, covering the whole range of family work. The ultimate perfection of a

SIMPLE FAMILY SEWING MACHINE.

Best Ornamentation. Complete Attachments. Full line of Stylish Cabinet Work.
Those in want of a first-class machine will find it to their interest to Call on or Address

JAMES H. BENEDICT, - **UNADILLA, N. Y.**

PAST COMMANDERS.

R. M. Rose,   G. D. Bartlett,   H. C. Richmond.

LIST OF MEMBERS.

Bartlett, George D, ...G, 1st N. Y. Eng.
Chappell, Erastus,..............................L, 1st N. Y. Reg.
Crawford, Lewis, ...E, 89 N. Y.
Edson, Joseph,....................................I, 121 N. Y.
Garlick, Ransler,...................................C, 114 N. Y.
Hopkins, Lewis,................................G, 1st N. Y. Eng
Packer, David E.,..............................E, 121 N. Y.
Potter, Emery,....................................B, 31 N. Y.
Rifenberg, William H.,.........................H, 144 N. Y.
Rose, R. M.,.....................................G, 1st N. Y. Eng
Rose, George W.,...............................D. 193 N. Y.
Tarbox, William A ,............................G, 192 N. Y.
Woodcock, James, ...H. 121 N. Y.
Whitney, Dustin W.,...........................G, 144 N. Y.
Weidman, Ralph,................................I, 76 N. Y.
Wellman, Horace,.............................M, 3d N. Y. Art.
Winser, Daniel G.,.............................E, 121 N. Y.
Wellman, Alonzo,..............................H, 152 N. Y.
Vandeusen, John,.............................A, 152 Mtd. Rifle.

IN MEMORIAM.

Aplin, Samuel C.,..............................I, 6th N. Y. C.
Holister, Leroy,.................................I. 121 N. Y.
Keith, Eligah,....................................152 N. Y.
Keith, Amos,....................................152 N. Y.
Keith, Charles,..................................152 N. Y.
Teller, Rev. D. M.,.............................H, 152 N. Y.
Rose, Freeman P.,.............................I, 121 N. Y.
Thorn, A. J.,....................................G, 6th N. Y. Cav.

Henry Saunders

DEALER IN

Books and Stationery,
PAPER HANGINGS,
PICTURES, -
FANCY GOODS, &C.

190 MIAN ST.,
Oneonta, - N. Y.

W. L. BROWN,

DEALER IN

Hardware, Stoves, Lamps, Fine Cutlery, Paints, Oils, Etc.

PLUMBING, STEAM AND GAS FITTING.

CORNER MAIN AND DEITZ STREETS,

ONEONTA, - - New York.

SPECIAL ATTENTION GIVEN TO ESTIMATES ON JOB WORK.

Brown Post, No. 15,

SCHENEVUS, N. Y.

Regular meetings first and third Thursday of each month at G. A. R. Hall.

BROWN Post was organized in March, 1874. Charter received March 11th and mustered into the department of New York March 24, 1874, E. D. Farmer Post, No. 119, Oneonta, N. Y., convening in special meeting for this purpose at Schenevus, with R. L. Fox, Commander, as mustering officer, assisted by James Roberts, S. V., E. J. Bixby, J. V., and other comrades from that post.

The Post was named in honor of Ziba and Hamilton Brown, two gallant soldiers, two honored sons of the town of Maryland, who did splendid service for the cause which they loved so well.

Hamilton Brown was born in the town of Maryland July 29, 1830. After attending common school went to Hartwick Seminary, and in 1884 entered Union Collage, graduating in the class of 1852. After graduating he entered the office of Judge Ferry at Schenevus and in 1854 became the junior member of the law firm of Ferry & Brown. In 1857 young Brown, who had already won marked distinction and wide renown as one of the most scholastic and profound of the younger members of the Bar of Central New York, entered into partnership with the distinguished lawyer, Horace Lathrop, under the firm name of Lathrop & Brown. The firm were enjoying a

Mrs. H. E. Parmer,
FASHIONABLE MILLINER,
Stamping Done to Order.

Second Floor First National Bank Building,

ONEONTA, - New York.

☀ MRS. B. ACKLEY, ☀

No. 34 Elm St., ONEONTA, N. Y.

——) DEALER IN (——

CHOICE CUT FLOWERS AND GREENS

ALSO

Cut flower designs furnished at short notice.

U. A. FERGUSON,

DEALER IN

Fruits, Nuts, Confectionery, Tobacco and Cigars.

✦ A ✦ Full ✦ Line ✦ Of ✦ Smokers' ✦ Supplies. ✦

SODA WATER ON DRAUGHT.

9 Chestnut St., ONEONTA, N. Y.

large and lucrative practice, their clients being from all parts of the state. There were few whose prospects were as bright. He was a ready debater and, although a young man, was recognized as an orator of no mean pretentions, but his country was calling. He did not hesitate. Leaving his profession, home and friends, he enlisted as private Aug. 5, 1861, and was mustered in at Albany Aug. 12, 1861. In Sept., 1862, was commissioned 2nd Lieut. Came north to procure recruits for a regiment then being organized at Norfolk, enlisting forty men at Schenevus and fifty in Oneonta. Soon afterwards was promoted to 1st Lieut. and Dec. 23, 1863, was promoted to Major of 2nd U. S. Colored Cavalry. Was taken sick in January, returned home in March and died Oct. 24, 1864. Was buried at Schenevus, N. Y., his funeral being attended by many friends from the surrounding country.

Harvey W. Brown, first Commander, was born in the town of Maryland in 1828. Completing his education at the Hartwick Seminary, located on a farm, soon after engaging in the general mercantile business. The war had broken out, the first battle of Bull Run had been fought and lost, a defeat so crushing to the Union Armies as to cause depression but not discouragement. The third call for troops was issued and the response came from the people with an alacrity which told how determined was the resolution that the cause of the Union should yet triumph over its assailants. Among the first to respond to his country's call was Harvey W. Brown, leaving the plow and business behind. He enlisted Aug. 5, 1861, and was mustered into the service as 1st Sergeant Aug. 12, 1861, at Albany, N. Y. Was promoted in Dec. to 2nd Lieutenant, going to the front with his regiment and receiving his commission as 1st Lieut. in February, 1862. He was a born soldier, participating in the batties near

CONANT'S
Cheap Cash Grocery and Crockery Store.

Leads them all,
    Carries the largest stock,
        Keeps the best goods and
            Sells for less money

Than Any Other House in the City.

189 MAIN STREET,

Williams, N. C., October, 1862, Kingston, White Hall and Goldsborough Dec. 1862; Jacksonville and Trenton, N. C., in Jan. 1863; Sandy Ridge May 1, 1863; Warsaw July 14, 1863; Tarborough July 20, 1863 and Streets Ferry July 25, 1863. Promoted to Captain in the fall of 1862 and in Dec. 1863, was again promoted to Major and assigned to the 1st Reg. U. S. Cavelry, which was recruited at Norfolk, Va., by Hamilton Brown, Col. Cole and J. Gerrard. Their first march was to Petersburg. After the battle of Petersburg they joined the Army of Potomac, where they remained until after the surrender of Gen. Lee, when they were sent to Brazo and San Diago. While here Major Brown resigned October 17, 1865, his health not permitting him to remain longer in the service. Returned to Schenevus and was elected Sheriff of Otsego county in 1866. Has filled the office of Justice of the Peace and Justice of Sessions, besides being Supervisor of the town of Maryland. Was charter member of Brown Post and its Commander for two years, 1874 and 1875. Comrade Brown died Oct. 23, 1888, and was buried at Schenevus, N. Y., with military honors, the Brown Post and delegates from posts throughout the county attending in a body. He was a true friend and neighbor. His memory is cherished by all who knew him.

Warren Bennett, born in the town of Maryland July 11, 1840. After attending the common schools engaged in farming. Enlisted in August, 1861, in Co. D, 3d N. Y. C. and was mustered in at Albany, going from there to Washington. His record is that of his regiment: always at his post and engaging in all the hard fought battles in which this regiment had participated, and enduring its hardships. Sent to the general hospital at Point Lookout. Md., July 4, 1864; remained four weeks and then rejoined his regiment near Bermuda Hundred. Discharged in

WESLEY P. MORSE,

EX-CHAPLAIN DIVISION OF NEW YORK, S. V., U. S. A.

Mr. Morse has always taken a deep interest in any undertaking calculated to be beneficial to the soldier, and at the first opportunity became a member of the order of the Sons of Veterans. He has written much for the press, and is the author of several S. of V. songs, poems, etc. On Dec. 9th, 1890, he received from Col. Geo. Addington the appointment of Chaplain of the Division. He now holds the position of First Sergeant of Carlos Baldwin Camp, Groton, N. Y., and has for some time edited the Sons of Veterans department in the *Weekly Ithican*.

Dec. 1865, and returned to Maryland and went to farming. Joined Brown Post as charter member and was elected Commander for the years 1876 and 1877. Enlisted as a private and for distinguished service was promoted to Corporal.

George Bennett, born in the town of Maryland. Educated at common schools and at the age of seventeen years went to Fort Smith, Ark., in the employ of the Overland Stage Company. In Feb. 1861, after the state had first voted not to secede from the Union and before the second convention was called, at which time the state had decided to secede, while returning from a Union meeting to their boarding house, he and four other men were attacked by seven rebels and after a skirmish Bennett and another were taken prisoners before a jury at Coroners Court and held for murder, the others jumping upon stage horses and fled. Two of the rebels were killed. While before the Coroner's Jury a mob of rebels came with thirty-five feet of rope to hang the prisoners to a tree. Wm. Farmer, the other prisoner, from Central New York, ran and was shot. Bennett was retaken and while the rebels were in search of a tree, a dozen Union men who had started in pursuit, commanded them to halt. Realizing their position the rebels fled. The sheriff came up and Bennett was taken to jail, escorted by twelve friends. Remained here seven months. During his confinement he was asked to join the rebel ranks. Succeeded in getting released through a friend (a rebel) who took him to assist in buying horses for the Rebel Government. Remained here until after the battle of Pea Ridge. In the spring of 1862 went to Jefferson City and drove the general staff ambulance team until Dec. 1862. Returned to the town of Maryland, intending to

AMERICAN ❋ HOTEL,

Main St., Schenevus, N. Y.

≻ First-Class and Thoroughly Appointed Throughout. ≺

J. ✢ H. ✢ SIVER, ✢ Prop.

THE FAVORITE RESORT FOR COMMERCIAL MEN.

Accommodations for Both Man and Beast.

K. & S. FORMAN,
Cloak ✣ Manufacturers,

No. 170 Main St.,   ONEONTA, N.Y.

The Only Cloak Manufactury Between Albany and Binghamton.

Those wishing to purchase will find this the Cheapest place in the County to buy

Fancy Goods, Rugs, Lace Curtains, etc.

SATISFACTION GUARANTEED.

Large assortment on hand to select from.

go back to service, but was drafted in 1863, paid $300 for substitute and enlisted in Co. E, 1st N. Y. Eng., Sept. 2, 1864. Mustered in as a recruit at Norwich, N. Y. Joined regiment at City Point, Va., April 2, 1865. Lee surrendering came back to Richmond and rebuilt the Mayo bridge on the James river that had been recently burned. Mustered out at Richmond June 30, 1865, returned to Schenevus and went on a farm. Joined the Brown Post, June, 1874. Was elected Cammander to serve during the years 1882 and 1883. He was an exceedingly popular officer and the administration of the Post's affairs were in keeping with the sturdy manliness which he is known to possess. Has held the office of Senior Vice, Officer of the Day and Adjutant, and is still an active member of the Post. Now residing at Schenevus with his family, consisting of his wife, daughter, aged 24 and two sons aged 20 and 12 respectively.

Henry Palmer, Commander for 1887, was born in the town of Maryland June 13, 1843. Attended the common schools and after procuring his education located upon a farm. Like many of the volunteers of Otsego county, he left the farm for the field and enlisted Aug. 13, 1862, as private in Co. F, 121st N. Y. Vol. Mustered into the U. S. service at Herkimer, N. Y. Read the record of the 121st Regiment at Fredericksburg, Rappahanock Station, Gettysburg, Salem Hights, Spotsylvania, Cold Harbor, Fisher Hill, Petersburg and Cedar Creek, participating in all the engagements and skirmishes of his regiment, their record becomes his record. In the many hard fought battles in which he participated he displayed undoubted courage and devotion for the cause he had espoused. Discharged June 25, 1865, returned to the town of Maryland, and joined the Post in 1874 and was Adjutant for several years. His administration was such as to receive

P. R. YOUNG,
PHOTOGRAPHER.

Oneonta, Headquarters.

Sidney, open Wednesdays.

Schenevus, open Fridays.

We do all Branches in our line. - - -
 - - Aiming at Excellence and Durability.

the approval of his comrades. He is now the efficient Quarter Master of the Post. Was Assessor for the town of Maryland for eight years, and is now residing near Schenevus, N. Y., respected by many kind friends and neighbors.

The present Commander, I. E. Hynds, was first elected in Dec. 1889, and is now serving his third term. He was born at Hyndsville, Schoharie county, N. Y. In 1860 went to Troy, N. Y., to learn the tinsmith trade, leaving the bench to go to the front. He enlisted Sept. 8, 1863, as private in Co. F, 21st N. Y. Cav., and was mustered into the U. S. service Sept. 18, 1863 as corporal, going to the front and participating in all the battles and skirmishes in which his regiment engaged. There are few who will forget the glorious record of the 21st N. Y. Cav. You will remember them at Charleston under Seigle, at New Market and with Gen. Hunter from Winchester to Lynchburg, meeting Gen. Early who had been reinforced by Longstreet. Here the Union troops were defeated and returned to the Union lines at Kanawha Valley, W. Va. Ordered from there to Parkersburg to assist in driving Early from Pennsylvania. The Regiment, being reduced from 1,200 to 200 men, was ordered to Cumberland to recruit. Then reporting to Gen. Sheriden in the Shanandoah, crossing the river and through Ashby's Gap, headed off Early's wagon train. When entering the Shanandoah side of the Gap they were fired upon by a superior force of rebels, losing seventy-five men. The Regiment made a splendid charge across the river, surprising the enemy and capturing many prisoners. During this charge Hynds' horse was shot from under him, but by swimming and through the assistance received by clinging to the tail of a horse he safely reached the shore, going into winter quarters at Winchester, having participated in twenty-eight hard fought battles in one year. War clos-

$10.00!

THIS IS WHAT CAN BE SAVED BY BUYING A

✻SEWING MACHINE✻
——)OF(——

V. S. FULLER, :-: OTEGO, N. Y.

WE DO NOT CLAIM IT THE BEST BUT WE **DO** CLAIM THERE IS
NO BETTER FAMILY SEWING MACHINE
ON THE MARKET THAN THE

✻ NEW ✻ HOME! ✻

Warranted for 5 Years!   *Light Running!*   *Try One!*

☞ Get our prices and save money.

ed, was ordered to Washington, thence to Fort Leavenworth, to the scene of hostilities on the part of the Indians, escorting Gov. Yates to the Rocky Mountains to treat with the Indians. Discharged at Leavenworth, August 31, 1866, being the last volunteer regiment in the U. S. service. Went to Cobleskill and completed his trade. In In 1869 went to Maryland and in 1872 removed to Schenevus and worked at his trade for two years, when he embarked in the general hardware business as the senior member of the firm of Hynds & Becker, where he is at the present writing located. Joined Brown Post Nov. 26, 1885; held the office of Senior Vice for two years and was elected Commander to serve during the year 1890, applying the discipline acquired by his splendid service on the field to the administration of his office. The Roster of the Post (which showed 27 members when he entered upon the duties of his office) had doubled at the end of his term. He was again elected for 1891 and re-elected to serve during the present year, the Roster of the Post now showing a membership of 58 in good standing. These satisfactory results are due entirely to his energy, influence and interest taken in the affairs of the Post. It is through his efforts and perseverance that the Post have procured the foundation and two bases for a Soldiers' Monument.

He was post master four years during Cleveland's administration, is a member of the Susquehanna Valley Lodge, No. 592, F. & A. M., and is at present residing with his family, consisting of a wife and two children, ages respectively 18 and 12, on Main street Schenevus.

Since the above was written Comrade Hynds has sustained an irreparable loss in the death of his beloved wife. Comrades and friends will extend to him their sympathy. Hearts will ache to hear of her passing away, but only the rememberance of her excellence and worth, and the

MRS. N. E. SMITH,

Ladies ✻ Hairdressing ✻ Parlor.

Bangs Cut and Trimmed, Hair Shampooed, Bleached, Colored and Dressed. Combings made up in front. Switches and Wigs, also Manicure.

178 MAIN STREET,   (up stairs,)   ONEONTA, N. Y.

LARD.   **GEORGE W. SHERMAN, SR.**   POULTRY.

 Meat Market.

The Choicest cuts of all kinds of

⭑ Fresh ✻ and ✻ Salt ✻ Meats. ⭑

CANED GOODS ALWAYS ON HAND.

Main, Street   ∴   OTEGO, N. Y.

⇒ E. ✦ E. ✦ BOWEN, ⇐

DEALERS IN

HARNESS, ROBES, BLANKETS, TRUNKS, HAMMOCKS, BAGS, WHIPS, DUSTERS, TOBACCO, CIGARS, GLOVES AND MITTENS.

Also a fine line of the

Burlington Patent Blankets.

MAIN ST., OTEGO, N. Y.

implicit faith she had in Him who doeth all things well, will give comfort and peace in the thought that Thy Will be done.

David Bostwick enlisted from the town of Maryland Feb'y 27, 1862, as private in Co. D, 3rd N. Y. C. Mustered at Albany, going to the front to Capitol Hill. He was with this famous regiment through all its marches, participating in all skirmishes and battles in which they were engaged and entitled to the honors given to the comrads of the gallant 3rd N. Y. Cav. Always at his post his record is that of his regiment. Discharged at City Point Dec. 2 and mustered out at Albany Dec. 27, 1865. Joined Brown Post in 1875.

The President issued the first call for troops April 15, 1861. The sun had hardly set on the day the news was received in the loyal town of Maryland until four of her sons had decided to respond and started for Albany by stage to enlist. One of those men was Jeremiah M. Davis. born at Milford, Otsego Co., N. Y., Feb'y 9, 1836. Educated at the district schools and engaged in the comon avocations of life until he enlisted at Albany April 29. 1861, as private in Co. F, 34th N. Y. Vol. Ordered to Washington, to Kalarama Heights, to Seneca Mills, thence to Poolville, Md., and on Oct. 1 to Edward's Ferry, where they engaged in battle at Balls Bluff under Gen. Stone; thence to Harper Ferry, to Winchester and back to Washington, to Fortress Monroe, with Gen. McClellan in the Peninsulla, the company being in the rear guard at the seven day's fight, until at Malvern Hill they were ordered to Harrison Landing and detailed from the regiment to convey prisoners to Portsmouth Grove July 10. Back just in time to participate in the battle of Antietam. After this battle followed Lee to Warrenton. While at War-

A. + E. + NYE,
General Baker,
AND DEALER IN
Plain and Fancy Cakes, Confectionery, Oysters and Crackers.

106 Main St., - ONEONTA, N. Y.

A. C. Bouten,
CARPET BEATING AND STEAM CLEANING.

Carpets called for and delivered within the Corporation limits.

Manufacturer of Cigar Boxes.
Lables Furnished if Desired.

32 Mechanic St., - Oneonta, N. Y.

One of the Best
Meat, Poultry, Fish, Fruit and Vegetable,
MARKETS IN ONEONTA.

Corner Main and Broad Streets, |-| C. SPENCER, Prop.

renton McClellan was released and Burnside took command. From here went to Washington, thence to Falmouth, opposite Fredericksburg, and four weeks after fought the battle of Fredericksburg. After the battle returned to camp doing picket duty. May 3 the 2nd division was transferred to 6th Corps under Gen. Sedgwick. Charged and captured Maryee Heights. After the fight they were relieved by the 121st Regiment and mustered out of service June 15, 1863. Aug. 24, 1864, he re-enlisted in Co. I, 51st Reg. N. Y. V. Sept. 1, 1864, left for the front as a veteran. Joined the regiment Sept. 7, commissioned Sargeant Sept. 10 and engaged in battle at People's Farm, was taken prisoner and sent to Salisbury, N. C. Remained here until March 2, 1865, with thirty-two others, only three of whom lived, and two died soon after they reached home, from starvation. Three weeks after he returned he recognized his people. Was wounded at Antietam in the arm, at Malvern Hill in the head and at Fredericksburg in the knee, each time refusing to go to the hospital. He is a charter member of Brown Post and takes a lively interest in its affairs.

OFFICERS OF BROWN POST.

I. E. Hynds,................Commander.
J. H. Grady,...............Senior Vice-Commander.
M. Knapp,..................Junior Vice-Commander.
J. Bates,......................Adjutant.
H. Palmer,..................Quartermaster.
S. L. Kelly,..................Chaplain.
Dr. Truman Iris,..........Surgeon.
Milo Kelly,..................Officer of the Day.
J. H. VanZant,............Officer of the Guard.

PAST COMMANDERS.

Harvey W. Brown,   Warren Bennett,   F. H. Cleveland,

E. S. GRIFFIN,

CASH BOOT AND SHOE STORE,

289 MAIN ST., UNADILLA, N. Y.

Boots, Shoes, Rubbers, &c.

The Largest Stock,

The Lowest Prices.

Call and Examine our Specialties in

LADIES, MISSES AND GENTLEMANS FINE SHOES.

T. DIBBLE & SON,

JEWELERS.

A FINE LINE OF GOLD AND SILVER WATCHES, CLOCKS,

JEWELRY, Etc., Etc.

Rings in Diamond, Opal, Garnet, Ruby and Pearl in Solid Gold,

ALSO 18 CARAT SOLID GOLD RINGS.

Rogers' Bros. Plated Ware.

REPAIRING AND CLEANING DONE AND WARRANTED.

Mulford & Siver Blk.,   Unadilla, N. Y.

A. E. Talmadge,   George Bennett,   D. D. Greene,
Milo Kelly,   Peter H. Kipp,   W. S. Hotchkin.
W. H. Chamberlin.   Henry Palmer,   J. K. Tyler,
S. L. Kelly,   I. E. Hynds,   A. M. Howard.

List of Members.

Barnes, Thomas S., ...I, 20 N. Y. C.
Bates, A. J., ...10 N. Y. H. A.
Barnes, Jerry P., ...D, 3d N. Y. C.
Bennett, George, ...E, 1st N. Y. Eng.
Butts, Geo. W., ...E, 1st N. Y. Eng.
Baldwin, Almond, ...F, 101 N. Y.
Bennett, Warren, ...D, 3d N. Y. C.
Chase, Robert, ...D, 3d N. Y. C.
Conover, Milton, ...D, 3d N. Y. C.
Cady, John, ...G, 1st N. Y. Eng.
Chase, David ....C, 51 N. Y.
Chamberlin, William, ...D, 3d N. Y. C.
Chase, Jerry, ...E, 1st N. Y Eng.
Chase, Miles, ...D, 3d N. Y. C.
Chamberlin, William H., ...E, 1st N. Y. Eng.
Cleveland, F. H., ...G, 3d N. Y. C., F 34 N. Y.
Davis, Jerry M., ...I, 51 N. Y.
Darling, Wm. H., ...G, 121 N. Y.
Dunham, H. P., ...I, 71 N. Y.
Dunham, Ephriam B., ...D, 3d N. Y.
Glassfield, L., ...E, 1st N. Y. Eng.
Glassfield, S. W., ...E, 1st N. Y. Eng.
Greene, D. D ,......................................G, 1st N. Y. Eng.
Gurney, John J., ...D, 3d N. Y. C.
Grady, James H., ...C, 61 N Y.
Howard, Perry, ...B, 4th N. Y.
Hynds, I. E ,.......................................F, 21 N. Y. C.
Hull, H. B., ...D, 3d N. Y. C.
Iris, Truman, ...E, 1st N. Y. C.

C. P. WAIT,
Furniture * and * Undertaking,
Main St., Otego, N. Y.

Parlor and Chamber Suits, Fancy Rockers, Window Shades, Pictures and Frames.

FRANK E. GRIFFIN,
PIANO TUNER AND ACTION REGULATOR,
Wells Bridge, N. Y.

Pianos, Organs.

Jones, J. J., ... I, 51 N. Y.
Kelly, Milo, ... E, 1st N. Y. Eng.
Kelly, S. L., ... E, 1st N. Y. Eng.
Knapp, Mordica, ... D, 3d N. Y. C.
Kipp, Peter H., ... 1 U. S. S. S.
Kildee, James, ... D, 3d N. Y. C.
Lewis, Joe, ... D, 3d N. Y. C.
Martin, James, ... F, 1st R I.
Nellis, Norman, ... I, 51 N. Y.
Olmstead, Derious .... D. 3d N. Y. C
Peaslee, Thomas, ... E. 69 N Y.
Page, Thomas, ... I, 51 N Y.
Palmer, David A., ... E. 1st N Y Eng.
Palmer, Henry, ... F. 121 N. Y.
Pratt, David, ... G, 1st N. Y. Eng.
Rider, Silas, ... H, 152 N. Y.
Rider, John F., ... H, 3d N. Y. C
Smith, Joseph H., ... D, 19 U. S. Inf.
Smellen, John J., ... D, 3d N. Y. C.
Spencer, John N. .... D. 3d N. Y. C.
Talmadge, Adelbert E, ... D, 3d N. Y C.
Thompson, Augustus E., ... B, 3d N. Y C.
Tompkins, Austin, ... G, 1st N. Y. Eng.
Tompkins, Samuel, ... G. 1st N. Y Eng
Tompkins, John, ... D. 2d N. Y. C.
VanZant, Joseph H , ... G, 1st N. Y. Eng.
Woodcock, Delos H , ... F. 121 N. Y.
Woodcock, George, ... I, 51 N Y.
Webster, D. W., ... E. 1st N. Y. Eng.

WINNE ✳ HOUSE,

GENESEE ST.,   (oppo. depot)   CHERRY VALLEY, N. Y.

FRANK WINNE, Prop.

Conveniently Located.   -:-   Near Business Part of Town.

COMMODIOUS SAMPLE ROOMS FOR COMMERCIAL MEN.

RATES: $1.50 PER DAY.

First-Class Accommodations for Permanent and Transient Guests.

The Bar always well stocked with Choice Wines, Ales, Beer, Liquors and Cigars.

C.J. Warner,   **WARNER BROS.**   F.B. Warner.

DEALERS IN

General Merchandise, Hardware, Tin, Copper and Sheet Iron Ware, Stoves, Groceries, Etc. Confections, Glass Ware, Tobacco and Cigars, Salt and Dried Meats. Canned Goods,

GENERAL REPAIRING, ROOFING, ETC., ETC., ETC.

East Worcester, N. Y.

In Memoriam.

Brown, Harvey W., Major..................D, 3d N. Y. C.
Dykeman, John..........................G, 1st N. Y. Eng.
Howard, Albert..........................G, 1st N. Y Eng
Hubbard, John,..........................G, 1st N. Y. Eng.
Kelly, Almond,..............................I, 51 N Y
Martin, James,..........................F, 1st R. I.
Preston, Peter..........................D, 3d N. Y. C.
Post, John,.............................I, 152 N. Y.
Sperry, R. E.,..........................I, 51 N. Y.
Woodcock, Gilbert,......................I, 51 N. Y.

Graves Decorated by Brown Post, No. 15.

REVOLUTION, 1776.

Stephen Brown,   Joel Martin.

WAR OF 1812.

Cass, Silas.   Chase, Willard,   Chase, Samuel,
Dunham, Jessie,   Houghton, Daniel.   Hallock, Daniel.
Spencer, William, Sperry, Peter.   Tompkins, Neamiah.

WAR OF 1861—1865.

Brown, Ziba H., died at Poolville, Va.,..........D, 3d N. Y C.
Brown, George F., killed in battle,..............D, 3d N. Y. C.
Banker, Wm. H.,....Killed at Ronoke Island, Feb. 8th, 1863.
Banker, Jessie....Killed at Fredericksburgh, Feb. 13th, 1863.
Banker, F. ., killed at battle of Wildnerness, June 25, 1864.
Bliven, W Sturart,...........................E, 1st N. Y. Eng.
Butts, Jacob,...................................Unknown.

Brownell, Charles, ...D. 3d N. Y. C.
Brown, Thadius C., ...D, 3d N. Y. C.
Boardman, Edwin, ...F, 121 N. Y.
Brown, Harvey W., Major......................D. 3d N. Y. C.
Brown, Hamilton,.................................D, 3d N. Y C.
Barnes, Elery ....D, 3d N. Y. C.
Crippen, Amos H.,................................E, 1st N. Y. Eng.
Cass, George L.,..................................D, 3d N. Y. C.
Chamberlin, John..................................D. 3d N. Y. C.
Chamberlin, Myron, killed at South Mountain,...I, 51 N. Y.
Chase, Brazilla,....................................Unknown.
Conover, C. C. B.,................................D, 3d N. Y. C.
Chamberlin, Lorenzo,.............................I, 51 N. Y.
Cyphers, James,...................................D, 3d N. Y C.
Chamberlin, Henry, died in prison,............I, 51 N Y.
Dolan, Lary,..I, 51 N. Y.
Fields, Randolph...................................18 N. Y.
Fellows, Wm A.,..................................Unknown.
Green, D. H.,......................................D, 3d N. Y. C.
Grady, John O ,..................................D, 3d N. Y. C.
Hubbard, John,....................................E, 1st N Y. Eng.
Hanor, John,.......................................G, 3d N. Y. C.
Hoose, Wilson,....................................Unknown.
Howard, A. M.,...................................Unknown.
Houghton, Seward, killed in battle,...........51 N. Y.
Hummell, Menzo,................................D, 3d N. Y. C.
Hoose, Reuben,...................................F, 121 N. Y.
Kelly, S. B.,.......................................M, 3d N. Y. L. A.
Kelly, Almond....................................F, 121 N. Y.
Keegan, Micheal,.................................D, 3d N. Y. C.
Lewis, Nelson, died in Libby Prison,.........D, 3d N. Y. C.

Lamphier, Orson,...I, 51 N. Y.
Logan, James E, shot in prison,.....................Unknown.
Manzer, Alfred H.,..Unknown.
Merrihew, Charles,..Unknown.
Moore, George, killed in battle,......................21 N. Y. C.
Post, John,...Unknown.
Peaslee, John,...Unkown.
Prindle, Philo,..51 N. Y.
Peaslee, Horace B., killled in battle,...............Unknown.
Sperry, R. E.,..I, 51 N. Y.
Seward, Charles H.,..Unknown.
Smallen, Frank B., killed in battle,...........D, 3d N. Y. C.
Tipple, Edgar,...Unknown,
Townsand, Charles,.....................................D, 3d N. Y. C.
Tiel, David H.,..D, 3d N. Y. C.
Talmadge, John M., ...E, 1st N. Y. Eng.
Thompson, John,..................................E, 1st N. Y. Eng.
Wright, Armstrong,..............................E, 1st N. Y. Eng.
Wilber, George L.,.......................................D, 3d N. Y. C.
Warrener, Charles, killed in battle,..............F, 121 N. Y.
Williams, E. O...D, 3d N. Y. C.
Winchal, Philemon,..................................Died in prison.
Wade, H. L.,..Died in hospital.
Wilber, Abram,...D, 3d N. Y. C.

Live and Let Live!

D. IVES,

MAIN STREET,   (Keyes Blk.)   WORCESTER, N. Y.

Staple and Fancy Groceries, Confections,

DRY GOODS, CROCKERY AND NOTIONS.

Hats, Caps, Stationery and School Supplies.

FRUITS, VEGETABLES, DRIED AND SALT MEATS.

5, 10 AND 15 CENT COUNTERS.

Cash Paid for Butter and Eggs.

To Comrades of the G.A.R.

AND TO THE PUBLIC.

The Best and Cheapest place in the County

— TO BUY —

CHOCE ✢ GROCERIES

— INCLUDING —

Teas, Coffees, all kind Canned Goods,

TOBACCOS, CIGARS, NOTIONS. &C.,

— IS AT —

J. C. MAGEE'S,

Main Street,   ∴   Worcester, N. Y.

Johnson Post, No. 25,

WORCESTER, N. Y.

Regular meetings second and fourth Wednesday of each month at G. A. R. Hall.

THE charter for this Post was received April 8, 1879, and organized and mustered into the department of New York April 22, 1879 by mustering officer L. Coe Young, of Binghamton, assisted by comrades from E. D. Farmer Post, Oneonta and Brown Post, of Schenevus.

The Post was named in honor of Capt. David I. Johnson, of Co. I, 51 N. Y. V., one of the truest and bravest soldiers of the 51st regiment. He came to Worcester in Sept. 1861 to enlist a company and when the officers were to be commissioned, an endeavor was made (which nearly succeeded) to commission as captain one who had influence, but had taken no part in raising the company and had no interest in common in those who composed its members. This failed, however, when Dr. Wm. H. Leonard, a member of the company, had stated the facts in the case to Gen. Yates. A commission as captain was at once given David I. Johnson. He was one of the most active men of the regiment and it was a pleasure to associate with him as a soldier, always at his post and looking to the interest of his men. He served faithfully until the battle of Newbern March 14, 1862, while leading his men to battle, with sword in hand and a red sash tied around his body, he was shot by a sharp shooter and died the next day. His remains were sent to New York and

Central House,

WORCESTER, N. Y.

SQUIRE SHAFER, Manager.

❧ A First-class House, Ably Managed. ❧

Free 'Bus to and From all Trains.

ELECTRIC BELL IN EVERY ROOM.

SAMPLE ROOM AND BATH ROOM.

❋ A DELIGHTFUL PLACE TO SPEND THE SUMMER. ❋

FIRST-CLASS LIVERY CONNECTED.

HOTEL CONNECTED BY WIRE WITH WESTERN UNION TELEGRAPH OFFICE.

THE TABLE IS THE SUBJECT OF TENDER REGARD BY THE PROPRIETOR.

buried in Greenwood, borne by sturdy hands and followed by many friends, one more of God's heroes was carried to his grave, leaving the memory of his fidelity and greatness as a heritage to his surviving comrades and friends.

Alfred Foland, elected to fill the unexpired term of P. P. Bentley, was born at Cherry Valley, N. Y., Aug. 8, 1844, and while completing his education at the academy at that place he enlisted as private in Co. H, 76 N. Y. V., and was mustered into service at Cherry Valley Jan. 6, 1862, going from here to Albany and arriving at Washington in March. He was as brave a soldier as ever shouldered a gun, serving with great courage and devotion to duty with his regiment on every bloody battle field from Rappahannock Station to the surrender of Lee at Appomatox, engaging in twenty-six hard fought battles. Read the history of this famous regiment at South Mountain, Antietam, Fredericksburg and the last desperate charge at Chancellorsville; read it at Gettysburg or in the Wilderness, Spotsylvania, Coal Harbor and Petersburg and you have the record of Comrade Foland. Always first with his regiment, enduring its hardships on the weary march and on the bloody battle field and entitled to its honors. Enlisting as private, promoted to Corporal, Sargeat and was discharged from this regiment as First Sargeant at Culpeper Jan. 6, 1864. He had in the meantime enlisted Jon. 1, 1864, as First Sargeant in Co. C, 147 N. Y. V., receiving a slight wound at the battle of Hatche's Run, the first battle in which he had participated with this regiment. June 1 was transferred to the 91st N. Y. V. Discharged near Washington Jan. 26, 1865, by reason of being rendered supernumary by the consolidation of the 147th and 91st. Returned to Worcester and went on to a farm. In 1886 engaged in the marble business and in 1889 went into the feed, flour and grain business. Was char-

D. E. SULLIVAN,

DEALER IN

GENERAL MERCHANDISE, JEWELRY, WATCHES, CLOCKS AND STATIONERY, CHOICE CONFECTIONS, COTTONS, FLAVORING EXTRACTS.

WATCHES, CLOCKS AND JEWELRY REPAIRED.

EAST WORCETER, New York.

L. J. BARNES,

ATTORNEY AND COUNCELLOR AT LAW,

PENSION AND CLAIM AGENT.

MAIN STREET, (Knapp Bl'k.) WORCESTER, N. Y.

KNISKERN + HOUSE,

C. B. KNISKERN, Proprietor.

RATES: $1.50 PER DAY.

Conveniently Located.   -:-   In Business Part of Town.

First-Class Accommodations for Perminent and Transient Guests.

Three Minutes walk from Depot.

MILFORD,   .:.   New York.

ter member of Post and upon its organization was elected Quartermaster, serving three months, when he resigned and was elected Commander in 1879 to serve during the unexpired term of P. P. Bently, who had resigned. His administration was such as to receive the hearty approval of its members, and he was again elected Commander to serve during 1882.

Charles Childs, born at Worcester Nov. 13, 1843. Attending the common schools and afterwards found employment as a clerk. He enlisted Oct. 9, 1861, in Co. I. 51 Reg. N. Y. V. January 7, 1862, left Annapolis on board the troop ship Lancer with his regiment for Roanoke Island, under Gen. A. E. Burnside. The transportation furnished by the Government was inadequate for the number of troops in the expedition, necessitating the crowding of the men, the 51st being placed in the hold of the ship and for four weeks confined where fresh air was unknown, without cooked food, the rations being simply hard tack and coffee and water in kerosene barrels to drink. Here the germs of disease which undoubtedly terminated his life were laid. He left the ship to take part in the battle of Roanoke Island Feb. 14, 1862, where he helped to win for his regiment the soubrequet by which it was ever known—the fighting 51st. March 14 he was again on the bloody battle field at Newbern, where every third man or officer was either killed or wounded, his company losing Capt. Johnson and First Lieut. Allen and Sargeant Cyrus Powers, with a score of brave men. With his regiment at Cedar Mountain, Kelly's Ford, White Sulpher Springs and up the Rapahannock, for three weeks almost constantly under fire, culminating in the second battle of Bull Run, in the retreat upon Washington, the march through Maryland to meet Gen. Lee at the battle of South Mountain, where he left the ambulance to join

FLINT & TAYLOR

—LEADING—

✷ CLOTHIERS ✷

FINE CUSTOM WORK

A SPECIALTY.

Gents' ✳ Furnishing ✳ Goods,

Dry and Fancy Goods,

LADIES'

Cloaks ✳ and ✳ Jackets,

Etc., Etc.

G. A. R. Uniforms and Hats.

in the fight, and on the march to Antietam, unable to walk he rode in the ambulance, though sick, he refused to leave the regiment until Lee was driven back south of the Potomac. At the battle of Antietam he was again found in the front of his regiment, all day under fire. late in the afternoon crossing the stone bridge in that brilliant charge made by the second brigade and 9th army corps, for two long hours holding the ground, thus gained in the face of a large force of the enemy, without a single round of amunition in the cartridge boxes, before the amunition train could be got up. Here closed his splendid military record. Health entirely broken down he was sent to Anapolis hospital, Md., and from there discharged and brought home by his father, as it was believed at that time he was to die. After a struggle of more than two years he so far recovered as to be able to engage to some extent in business persuits. He became an active member of Johnson Post and served as Commander during the year 1884 and at the time of his death was Adjutant. Loved as a soldier by all his comrades, he will be sincerely mourned. Of all who enlisted in the defense of his country none were more brave or patriotic. Comrades who survive, for one of our number, taps have sounded. Let us cherish while life shall last his memory, and pray that should our country again need defenders her loving sons may emulate his virtues.

Perrin Waterman, born at Decatur Aug. 20, 1836. After receiving a common school education went on a farm and at the age of 16 years learned the painters trade. Enlisted as a private in Co. G, 121st Reg. N. Y. V., July 25, 1862. Engaged at the battle of Salem Church and under fire at Gettysburg. Soon after was detailed to the horse battery 2nd division U. S. Artilery to letter their wagons. Returned to regiment and detailed to division

Low Fares
TO THE
WEST.

"D. & H."

THE
DELEWARE & HUDSON RAIL ROAD

IS THE CHEAPEST AND THE FAVORITE ROUT TO ALL POINTS IN THE WEST.

For full Information, Rates, Time Tables, Tickets, etc., inquire of nearest "D. & H." Ticket Agent, or write to the undersigned,

J. W. BURDICK,
General Passenger Agent.

headquarters to letter tents and wagon trains. Joined regiment for the campaign of 1864. Was wounded at the battle of the Wilderness and sent to Fairfax Seminary hospital. Soon after granted a furlough for 30 days, returning to regiment in the Valley in July. Was here detailed to drive the ambulance, and carried Gen. Russell's body, who was killed at Winchester, to Harper's Ferry. Remained here until war closed, being discharged at Hall's Hill, Va., with the regiment. Returned to Decatur and finally to Worcester. Joined Johnson Post in 1869. Was elected Commander for 1885, at which time there was some talk of disbanding the Post but through his efforts the Post had regained its former standing. Living six miles from the place of meeting he was absent but once during his term of office.

Henry J. Goodrich, born at Worcester July 14, 1842. Educated at the district schools and located on a farm. Like many of the sons of Otsego, he left the plow to serve his country, enlisting as private in Co. I, 121st N. Y. V., and mustered into the service at Herkimer, N. Y., going to Washington and thence to Fort Lincoln, participating in the battle of South Mountain, and after battle of Antietam picked up the wounded. Going to Fredericksburg was sent to hospital at Berlin and from Berlin to Harper's Ferry and to Judiciary Square hospital at Washington and discharged on account of general disability. Is charter member of Johnson Post and served as Officer of Day for two years and elected Commander to serve during the year 1889.

Served as Poor Master of the town of Worcester for two years.

Hiram Mereness, born in the town of Roseboom, Otsego Co., his parents moving when he was a lad to Seward, N. Y. Attended the district school, going to Norwich in

Worcester Insurance Agency.

FIRE, LIFE, ACCIDENT AND WIND STORM INSURANCE.

A. PATRIDGE, AGENT.

Eight large Company's Represented. All loses Promptly paid.
Eighteen Years Experience. Solid Indemnity Given.
The Public Patronage Solicited.

B. Goodenough,

DENTIST,

MAIN ST., WORCESTER, N. Y.

GAS ADMINISTERED WHEN DESIRED.

W. S. WAGONER,

Tonsorial Artist.

Ladies' Curling, Shampooing and Childrens

WORK A SPECIALTY.

Shelland Block, :: Worcester, N. Y.

1860, where he completed his education and enlisted Sept. 24, 1862 as a private in Co. I, 152nd N. Y. V., and mustered into the service at Herkimer Oct. 9. Ordered to Chain Bridge, defense of Washington, doing guard duty while Early was raiding Pennsylvania. Sent to New York to hospital in July, 1863, thence to Brandy Station and from here to convalescent camp at Cumberland, Va. In October joined regiment near Brandy Station. Dec. 1863, crossed the Rappahannock and engaged in the battle at Miles Run, Wilderness, Spotsylvania, Cold Harbor, Petersburg, Deep Bottom, Lookout Mountain, North Anna, before Petersburg and at Reams Station. He was a brave soldier and is entitled to the honors of his regiment. Discharged July 26, 1865 and returned to Worcester. Joined Johnson Post and elected Commander for 1890. In the spring of 1865 removed to Decatur, where he is now residing with his family—wife and son William aged 25 and an adopted daughter aged 19.

William H. Leonard, born at Roxbury, Delaware Co., in 1835. Attended common schools, completing his education at the academy. Commenced the study of medicine and in 1854 graduated as a physician and surgeon. Enlisted Sept. 28, 1861 and mustered Oct. 9, 1861, as 2nd Lieut. in Co. I, 51st N. Y. V., and detailed for duty as acting assistant surgeon, and March 28, 1862, was commissioned assistant surgeon and in November of the same year was made surgeon of the regiment. There is not a brave man who served with the 51st Regiment that does not remember with as much gratitude and admiration the noble consecration to duty and its faithful performance by Dr. Wm. H. Leonard, the surgeon of the regiment, as he does, the most brilliant and dashing act of personal bravery. Returned to Worcester in 1863. Is a charter member and for one term surgeon of Johnson Post, a

Unadilla House,

MRS. TINGLEY, Proprietor,

Main Street, - Unadilla, N. Y.

THIS House has been Newly Furnished and Fitted throughout and ranks with the very few first-class Country Hotels. It is a favorable resort for Commercial Men and Summer Boarders, and a haven of satisfying and perfect rest for those who seek its hospitalities. Those who wish to enjoy the quiet of home life and the comforts of a first-class City Hotel, with pure wholesome food and delicacies in their season, with most delightful climate and pure air, will patronize this house. Fine Sample Rooms, Spacious Parlors and First class in every respect.

prominent Mason, member of Baptist church, an honored citizen and a respected neighbor.

Harrison Pettie, the present Commander of Post, was born at Westford, Otsego Co., April 29, 1841. Was educated at the common schools at that place. Leaving school he worked at the carpenter's trade and enlisted Oct. 1, 1861, as a private in Co. K, 76th N. Y. V., and mustered in at Cherry Valley in October, going to the front at once, engaging in the battles of Chancellorsville and Fredericksburg. He was wounded at the battle of Chancellorsville and sent to Douglas hospital, Washington and soon after sent to Central Park hospital. He never fully recovered from the effects of his injuries and was discharged for general disability Dec. 19, 1863. For two years after his discharge he was obliged to use crutches. Went west in December, 1864. In 1868 returned to Westford and removed to Worcester and joined Johnson Post in 1886. He was a good soldier and it was with regret that he was obliged to leave the service. He had six brothers in the army. One Rufus was killed at the battle of Roenoke and George killed at Gettysburg. He served as Senior Vice for several terms and was elected Commander to serve during 1892. He is a painstaking officer, and, although just commencing upon his term, his administration is meeting with the approval of its members and through his energy it is safe to say the Roster at the close of his term will show an encreased membership. While west he held the offices of Justice of the Peace and Deputy Sheriff of Stotts Co., Minn. Is of a quiet and reserved disposition, a true friend and neighbor.

Seth M. Flint was born at Berne, Albany Co., N. Y., Oct. 7, 1846, and while attending school at that place (when only fifteen years old) he decided to join the army.

Leaving school, friends and parents, walked to Albany, twenty miles, to enlist. He had given the matter much thought and contrary to the wishes and advice of friends (owing to his age) he decided to go. Fearing that there might be some objections to his going to the front on the part of his parents, he enlisted under the assumed name of Charles M. Seaver. The young hero was not mistaken for anxious friends had scanned the Recruiting Station closely, but in vain, for the enlistment of Seth M. Flint. Had it not been for this precaution, on his part, he would have been obliged to return with his parents. He enlisted July, 11, 1862, in Albany in the regular cavelry and after two month's drill at Carlisle, Pa., Barracks, was assigned to Co. H, 5th U. S. Cav., and served about one year as private, participating with the regiment in eighteen battles. The winter of 1862 and 1863 was a severe one and being almost constantly on duty, in the field and on the picket lines, exposed to severe weather without shelter, he contracted rheumatism. June, 1863, was sent to Alexandria, Va., for treatment, and not fully recovering he was allowed his choice, a discharge from the service or appointment to Bugler. Choosing the latter he returned to the regiment in September. Was subsequently assigned to Co. F, same regiment as Buglar, in which capacity he served until '64, when he was ordered to report to headquarters, Armies of the United States, as escort Bugler on Gen. Grant's staff from Culpeper, 1864, until the surrender of Gen. Lee at Appomattox April 9, 1865, and June 11 received his discharge from the service, having served three years. July, 1865, he entered the employ of Moore, Wilstach & Baldwin, publishers of the life of Abraham Lincoln, and in Feb'y, 1867, married Miss Kate M. Gifford, the accomplished daughter of Abraham Gifford, and engaged in farming in Rensselaerville, N. Y. In the year '69 he embarked in the mercantile business in same town, continuing the business until 1879, when he associated with him a former clerk, Mr. C. E. Taylor, and removed to Worcester, and under the firm name of Flint & Taylor, engaged in the clothing and furnishing business. They have since added a manufacturing branch to the business, and their merchant tailoring, as well as ready made work, has a wide and favorable reputation in Otsego and adjoining counties. Joined Johnson Post, Department of N. Y. G. A. R. Chosen Senior Vice Commander, and elected Commander to serve during the years 1886 and '87. His administration was such as to enhance the reputation of the post in the department, and he was again elected Commander for 1891. The soldiers monument fund society was organized during his administration. He also served on the Department staff during Gen. J. I. Sayles' administration in 1887. Is a member of Oak Hill Lodge, F. & A. M., No. 425, Greene Co., N. Y., always taking a lively interest in all that pertains to the welfare of the village of Worcester, and the advancement of good citizenship and American loyalty. He now resides with his estimable wife on Main St., Worcester, N. Y., one son, Abram G., residing in Fitchburg, Mass. The youngest son, Little Frankie, a bright lad of seven years, was laid away in the beautiful Maple Grove Cemetery, December 1884.

James Kniskern, born at Seward Valley, Schoharie Co., Aug. 23, 1840, and enlisted at Seward Sept. 1862. Mustered in at Albany, Oct. 9. Ordered to the front at Antietam, participating in the battles of Fredericksburg, Chancellorsville, Snicker's Gap, twice through Bull Run and Gettysburg. After the battle of Gettysburg, sent to convey wounded soldiers to Camp hospital. Camp breaking up rejoined his regiment and sent to Mt. Pleasant hospital tn Aug. 1863, and in January, 1864, sent to Bedlow Island, New York, then to distribution camp,

Alexandria, and soon after was transferred to the Veteran Reserve Corps at Langley to look after Mosby, remaining here until the surrender of Lee and the assassination of Lincoln, April 25. Discharged Jan. 5, 1865, at Washington, returned to Seward and to farming. In 1871 located at Cherry Valley and joined the Upton Post. Moved to Worcester in 1890, and joined the Johnson Post by transfer card from Upton Post, and is now serving his second term as Officer of the Guard.

Judson Goodenough, born Sept. 2, 1838, at Jefferson, Schoharie Co., N. Y. After receiving a common school education went on a farm. In the fall of 1860 commenced to work at the carpenter's trade. Enlisted Sept. 3, 1864, as a recruit for Co. B, 91st N. Y. V. Joined his regiment at Fort Henry, Baltimore. Feb'y, 1865, ordered to City Point, near Petersburg. Engaged in battle of South Side Rail Road, Five Forks and following Lee until he surrendered at Appomattox. After surrender of Lee marched to Richmond, thence to Farmville, where they received news of Lincoln's assassination. Going from Farmville to Arlington Heights and discharged June 10, 1865. Returned to Jefferson and removed to Worcester village in 1881 and in the spring of 1892 purchased a farm at Tuscan, one mile from the village of Worcester, where he has built a handsome residence, and is now residing with his family, consisting of wife and an accomplished daughter aged 21, now teaching school in the town of Worcester, N. Y.

John H. Groat, born at Worcester, N. Y. Enlisted as a recruit in Co. C, 3d N. Y. V. Joined regiment at Folly Island. Participated in battle in front of Petersburg, Cold Harbor, near White House landing and Chapin's Farm. Sent to hospital just before battle of Fort Fisher. Discharged June 10, 1865. Joined Johnson Post in the fall of 1891. He is now residing at East Worcester, N. Y.

Elijah B. Putnam, born at Root, Montgomery Co., Mch. 1, 1846. Went to Decatur when 10 years old. Enlisted in Aug. 1864. Mustered in at Norwich. Sent to Brooklyn and assigned to duty on the gun boat Kensington. Sailed for Beaufort, N. C. Transferred to the gun boat, Quaker City, with the North Atlantic Blockading Squadron. Engaged in the battle at Fort Fisher and afterwards went to Fort Monroe with wounded soldiers; thence to Mexico to the mouth of the Riogrand River, where they got three prizes, he receiving $46.64 prize money. Returned to New Orleans and discharged May 12, 1865. Is charter member of Post.

C. O. Waterman was born at Worcester in March, 1847, and was educated at the district schools. One bright Sabbath morning in August, 1864, he started for church, but controled by a patriotic desire to serve his country, he went to Oneonta and enlisted as a private in the 5th N. Y. Indipendant Battery Aug. 7. Was mustered into the service at Norwich and ordered to New York, thence to Heart's Island, joining the command in the Shanandoah Valley. Was with his battery, participating in its engagements and marches (though sick, refusing to go to the hospital) until they were discharged July 6, 1865. Returned to Worcester and went to Nebraska in 1874, retured to Worcester in 1881 and since then engaged in the grocery business. He Joined E. D. Farmer Post at Oneonta in 1870, and by transfer card from that post, joined Johnson Post in 1883, and has served as Quartermaster and adjutant of the post. He is a member of the Masonic Lodge, F. & A. M., of Schenevus, and a rrspected citizen of Worcester, N. Y.

John Lovejoy, born at Cherry Valley May 10, 1829.

DELLMER CRANDALL.

From its conception the business of this concern has been most successful and has steadily increased and extended until to-day it stands at the head of similar concerns in this vicinity. We are safe in asserting that the finest stock of Ready-made Clothing, Gents' Furnishing Goods, Hats, Caps, Boots and Shoes in Oneonta, can be seen at his new store, 144 Main street. Mr. Crandall, born in Chenango county, in 1862, first located in Oneonta in 1886, going into the Clothing and Boot and Shoe business in the Rockwell block Seeking more commodious quarters removed to the Westcott block. His health failing in June, 1890, went out of business for the time being. In May, 1891, he embarked again in the Boot and Shoe business, locating at 175 Main street. Here he did a fine business and in 1891 commenced the manufacture of Boots and Shoes for the wholesale and retail trade, this branch of the business proved a great success, his trade now extending through New York state, northern Pennsylvania and southern Ohio. His store at this time being inadequate for his steadily increasing trade he sought new quarters and April 1st, 1892, he removed to the commodious building, 144 Main street, occupying two floors—22x100 feet. The first floor is used as a sales room where can be found an elegant stock of Ready made Clothing, Gents' Furnishing Goods, Hats, Caps, Boots and Shoes, and four polite and attentive clerks catering to the wants of their numerous customers all under the personal supervision of Dellmer Crandall. Among the specialties are Ladies' Dongola, McKay Sewed, fine Shoes. Men's fine Calf Shoes from $2.00 to $3.00, Vica Kid and Genuine Kangaroo from $2.00 to $3.00. The basement is used for storing purposes and packing room. Mr. Crandall is assisted by his father, James H. Crandall, who has had 25 years experience, and is now connected with one of the largest Wholesale Clothing Houses in the trade, located on Broadway New York City, thus giving him a decided advantage over his competitors in buying, of at least 15 per cent. this he proposes to give to his customers. Honorable in all his dealings and by energy, enterprise and strict attention to business, he has built up his trade to its present magnificant proportions.

Educated at the common schools and went on to a farm. Moved to Decatur in 1859. Enlisted at Albany as private in Co. D, 10th N. Y. H. A. Mustered at Albany June 3, 1862, and ordered to Heart's Island, thence to Boliver Heights, Va., down the river to Berryville Pike and guarding wagon trains from there to Washington and crossed the Potomac to Alexandria and took transport to City Point, thence to Bermuda Hundred doing guard duty, to rebel lines at James Landing, remaining two months, when they drove the rebels through Petersburg. Discharged at Sacket Harbor, returned to Worcester, and joined Johnson Post as charter member and has served as Officer of the Guard.

Charles W. Smith was born in Germany. Coming to America when 3 years old and going on to a farm at St. Johnsville, Montgomery Co., N. Y., thence to Little Falls, Learned the butcher business and afterwards locating at Cooperstown, and enlisted as private in Co. D, 152 N. Y. V. Sept, 25, 1862, mustered at Mohawk and ordered to Camp Marshall, remained here until spring of 1863. His record is that of his regiment, going up the James river to White House Landing and wounded at the battle of the Wilderness. Discharged at Albany and returned to Cooperstown, moving to Richmondville, then back to Cooperstown, thence to Beaver Meadow, Chenango Co., to Oneonta, then to Rockwell Mills and locating at Worcester and opening a butcher shop in 1890. Joined Johnson Post, elected Sergeant and is at present Junior Vice Commander.

D. S. Smith, Born at Catskill June 30, 1843. Enlisted in Co. H, 144 as private, and mustered in as Corporal at Delhi, N. Y., remained with the regiment until they arrived at Hilton Head, when he was commissioned as 2nd Lieutenant and assigned to a company in the 103d Regi-

J. T. HADSELL & SON,

PROPRIETORS OF WORCESTER

STEAM SAW, PLANING AND FEED MILL

AND LUMBER YARD.

BUILDERS & CONTRACTORS

GENERAL REPAIRING OF ALL KINDS

A SPECIALTY.

Office and Mill, Depot St., near Depot,

WORCESTER, N. Y.

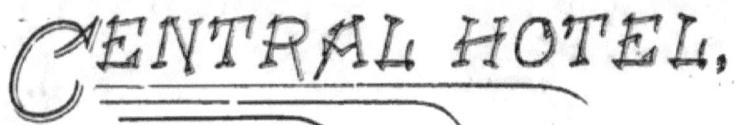 CENTRAL HOTEL,

AARON SALISBURY, PROPRIETOR.

First Class Accommodations for Permanent and Transient Guests.

Milford, N. Y.

The Leading Hotel of the Place.

Livery Attached.

NEW HOUSE.   NEWLY FURNISHED.

ment, U. S. C. T., Col. Woodford commanding. Was acting Quartermaster of post at Fort Rudeski and assistant commisary of substance. Discharged at Fort Rudeski, and mustered out at Savannah, Ga. After discharge located at Worcester, where he has since resided, his business being that of commercial traveler. In 1887 he received the nomination of County Clerk, of Otsego Co., on the Republican ticket.

Orlando Spurbeck, born at Richmondville, where he attended the district school, enlisting Aug. 23, 1862, as private in Co. G, 134th N. Y. V. Mustered into the U. S. service at New York; thence to the front. Was sick at Arlington Heights. With restored health he sought his regiment and was always on duty until wounded at the battle of Gettysburg in July, 1863, receiving three gun shot wounds, one in the right wrist, one in the left arm, requiring a resection of four inches, and one in the left leg below the knee. Sent to Jarvis hospital, where he contracted small pox. Sent to Marine Barricks, Baltimore and transferred to David's Island, New York, sent to Gen. Butler's Headquarters, Army of the James, as dispatch bearer and was again wounded in left hip at Welden Rail Road, the ball still remaining in the thigh. Sent to David's Island, New York, for treatment and discharged in June, 1865. He was a model soldier and one of those who can truly say "I have participated in a conflict, having no paralell since the world began." Joining the army full of life and vigor, he returns to his form r home in broken health, with the proud satisfaction that in the hour of his country's need, he had responded, did splendid service and made untold sacrificies, that his country might live.

Daniel Kaple was born at Decatur, Otsego Co., April 8, 1864. Received a common school education, and learned the carriage maker's trade. Enlisted as a recruit for Co. D, 10th N. Y. H. A., April 9th 1864. Joined the regiment at Hart's Island. In July ordered to Fortress Monroe aboard transports to Boliver Heights to Winchester, to front of Petersburg, near Bermuda Hundred, participating in the battle in front of Petersburg. During a charge at Bermuda Hundred, the 2d of April, at daybreak, he was, with three others of his company, taken prisoners and sent to Libby Prison, remaining until the morning of the day Richmond was surrendered, taking the prisoners with them and kept until the 9th of April. Lee surrendering they were released, joined regiment and discharged at Rome, June 9, 1865. Returned to Decatur and joined Post in 1880. Has served as chaplain of same.

M. D. Bentley was born Dec. 19, 1834, in the town of Westford, Otsego Co., and educated at the common schools and went on a farm. He enlisted in Co. D, 3d N. Y. C. under Capt. Brown, but was rejected by reason of poor sight. Enlisted the second time, was accepted and mustered in at Norwich, N. Y., Aug. 29, 1864 as a private in Co. E, 1st N. Y. Eng. Joined his company at Point of Rocks, Va., crossed the James and participated in the two day's fight in front of Richmond Sept. 28th and 29th. The regiment was in camp near here for one month at work in the canal near James Landing, and other work on the Dredge boats; then to City Point building levees, boarding on the Canal boats, going from here to Hatche's Run, to Farmville and then to Appomattox, where they remained until the surrender of Lee. Was on the field at Antietam, then back to Manchester and mustered out. Returned to Worcester and joined Johnson Post in 1887.

Charles Wilsey, born at Worcester in Oct. 1843. Received a common school education and enlisted as private in Co. I, 121st N. Y. V. Wounded at Salam Heights May 3, 1863, the ball passing through the right wrist at the joint. Sent to Mt. Pleasant hospital, remaining one year, when he was discharged. Returned to Worcester and went on a farm. Joined Johnson Post as charter member and has served as Junior Vice Commander. He is now residing at Schenevus, N. Y., in the employ of Markham & Reynolds.

A. D. Phillips, born at Harpersfield May 22, 1841. Attended school at South Worcester, and enlisted Aug. 30, 1862 in Co. F, 152 N. Y. V. Taken sick at the siege of Suffolk, sent to Mt. Pleasant hospital. Joined regiment at New York in June. He was a good soldier, his record being that of his regiment. After his discharge he returned to Worcester. Joined Johnson Post in 1890, and is now Sargeant of the post.

Simeon Welch, born in Schoharie Co., October, 1820. After leaving school, drove stage for 16 years, went on a farm. Enlisted Nov. 16, 1861 as private in Co. I, 51st N. Y. V. Mustered at New York, went to Annapolis, Md., Dec. 25, took vessel and engaged in the battle of Ronoke Island, on Feb'y 7, 1862; thence to Newbern City, N. C., engaged in battle and capture of Newbern; thence up to Culpeper Court House, and to second Bull Run, Aug. 27 and 29, and through Washington on the way to Antietam. Taken sick at Antietam, sent to Harwood tent hospital and transferred to Germantown Hospital, Philadelphia, and discharged Jan. 12, 1863, by reason of general disibility. Returned to Worcester and joined Post in 1890.

Daniel Sullivan, born at Roseboom, in August, 1830. His father and mother died when he was a lad. He was bound out and experienced all the hard knocks which usually are the result of an experience of this kind. He attended the common school at Oswego. When 19 years old left Oswego and attended school two years, learned the harness trade. Enlisted at South Valley Sept. 6, 1862, in Co. I, 152nd N. Y. V., as corporal. June 9, 1863, was detached as chief sadler of the Quartermaster Department under Geo. S. Dodge. Discharged July 13, 1865. In April, 1872, removed to East Worcester and embarked in the harness business. He is an honored citizen and of most excellent moral habits, a social companion of a quiet and reserved disposition. It is a satisfaction to give testimony of his worthiness. Joined post in 1887 and has held the office of Senior Vice Commander.

Perry Tripp was born at Otsego June 15, 1841, and enlisted as recruit for Co. D, 17th Penn. Cav., March 29, 1864. Was mustered in to the U. S. service at Troy, Bradford Co., Pa., going to Aquia Creek and joined the regiment in the Wilderness, participating in the battle of the Wilderness, including the seven day's fight; thence to Pamunkey River, below Petersburg, and back to Petersburg to re-enforce Sheridan in the Shanandoah Valley. Was wounded twice at the battle of Shepherdsville, Aug. 18, while charging on a wagon train, and sent to hospital at Winchester. Remained here until Sept. 18, and sent to Richmond as a prisoner, Oct. 8th was paroled and sent to Annapolis, Md., thence to Sandy Hook to dismounted camp. Was ordered Feb'y 29 with Sheridan to Petersburg, engaging in battle at Five Forks. Was taken prisoner, sent to Petersburg and back to Annapolis again, remaining here until discharged from the service. Returned to Worcester and in 1884 joined Johnson Post, and has served for one year as Junior Vice Commander.

Parmer Diefendorf was born at Middlefield July 4, 1842. His parents moving to Richmond when he was six years old. Attended the district schools and afterward learned the wagon making trade. He enlisted in August, 1864 as a recruit for Co. L, 3d N. Y. C. Joined the regiment at Bermuda Hundred, going to Mount Zion church and thence to Deep Bottom. His record is that of his regiment, until they were dischagred. A brave soldier, engaging in all the battles, marches and skirmishes, in which they were engaged from the time of his enlistment. Returned to East Worcester and joined Post in 1884, where he is now residing with his wife and three children.

I. S. Atkins was born in Schoharie Co., Jan. 3, 1837, going to Worcester when 9 years old. Educated at the Draper Institute, Westford, and accepted a position as clerk. Enlisted in August, 1864. Was mustered in to the service at Brooklyn, N. Y., and assigned to the steamer Malvern, flag ship, in the North Atlantic, Blockading Squadron, under Admiral Porter. He did active service up and down the James river. Engaged in battle at Fort Fisher, then up the James to Washington, N. C., and at the capture of Richmond. Discharged in June, 1865. Returned to Worcester and soon after went to Indiana, where he resided for ten years. Returned to Worcester and engaged in the furniture business for two years and in 1891 went in to the hardware business. Is a charter member and was for three years Adjutant of Johnson Post.

Daniel Ives, born at Stanford, Dutches Co., July 29, 1829. Moved to Otsego Co., when a boy and in 1845 to Broome Co. and in 1859 to Smithfield, Pa. Enlisted Oct. 1862, as private in Co. D, 16th Penn. Cavalry. Mustered into the service at Harrisburg Nov. 2. Engaging in the battles of his regiment until wounded and sent to hospital near Alexandria. Discharged Dec. 1865, at Elmira. In 1869 went to Union and in 1875 took up his residence at

J. M. MEAD,

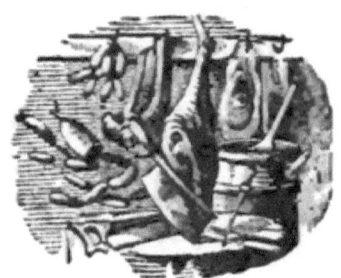

DEALER IN

Fresh & Salt Meats,

Poultry, Fish, Oysters and Game in their season

All kinds of Fruits and Vegetables in season.

Main St., East Worcester, N. Y.

Milford Jewelry Store,

L. E. SAXTON, Manager and Optician.

DEALER IN

Jewelry, Watches, Clocks, Guns, Sporting Implements, Musical Merchandise, &c.

R. A. PEARSE,

OPTICIAN,

Eyes with every variety of refractive errors skillfully treated and Satisfaction guaranteed.

EXAMINATION FREE!

WATCHES, CLOCKS AND JEWELRY REPAIRD AND WARRANTED,

MILFORD, - N. Y.

Binghamton and joined Watrous Post, No. 30, at that place. Went to Bainbridge in 1890 and removed in 1892 to Worcester. Always taking a lively interest in the G. A. R. and expects soon to become a member of Johnson Post at Worcester.

Aaron L. Putnam, born at Middlefield, Otsego Co., N. Y., in October, 1838. Was educated at the Hartwick Seminary, and enlisted Sept. 15, 1862, as private in Co. C. 152nd N. Y. V., and mustered into the service at Herkimer, N. Y. Was wounded at Weldon Rail Road June 22, 1864, and went to Finley Hospital, Washington, and promoted to Corporal. Remained here, where he was detailed to work in the carpenter shop until he was discharged June 14, 1865. Returned to South Valley and worked at the carpenter and joiner's trade until spring of 1867, went to Altona, Knox Co., Ill. Returned in September, 1889, to South Valley and in October, 1890, moved to Worcester, where he is now residing with his wife.

William H. Mallery, born in the town of Maryland, Feb. 20, 1844. Enlisted at Norwich Sept. 1, 1861, as a recruit for Co. E, 1st N. Y. Eng. Joined his company on Bermuda Front in the spring of 1865. Left Bermuda Front and went to Hatch Island, and after surrender of Lee marched back through Richmond to Petersburg, where the regiment built the Mayo bridge. Mustered out of the service at Richmond July 2, 1865. Returned to Maryland and embarked in the bee business. He has at the present writing more than 600 swarms of bees. Joined the post in 1880, always taking a lively interets in its welfare.

John K. Tyler was born at Westford, Otsego Co., N. Y., on the 6th day of March, 1843, and was educated at the common schools. After leaving school he taught one year, when he enlisted, Aug. 7, 1862, as a private in Co. D, 121 N. Y. V., and mustereed into the U. S. service at Mohawk, and promoted to Sergeant, and for bravery at the battle of Cedar Creek was again promoted to First Sergeant. He was one of four men selected to go ahead of the regiment as scouts on their way to Petersburg, and before daylight on the 3d day of April,1865, he was in the city. The venerable Gen. Upton remarked, (refering to Tyler) "that is a small man but it is hard to kill him." He was discharged at Halls Hill June 25, 1865. Returned to Westford and embarked in the general mercantile business, three years after going into the insurance business, taking up his residence in the village of Worcester in 1888. In giving the services of the many brave soldiers, who fought with the "Onesters," the marches, skirmishes and battles have been written and will become familiar to those who peruse the pages of this volume. The record of the 121st is the record of Comrade Tyler (he being away from his regiment but eleven days on a furlough) during his term of enlistment. There are none who will forget the splendid service rendered by the brave men of the 121st Reg. N. Y. V. He was a charter member of Brown Post, Schenevus, N. Y., and elected commander for one year. Taking a transfer card joined Johnson Post, No. 25, Worcester and served as Adjutant one year and is at present writing Sergeant Major. Since the war he has won marked distinction and wide renoun, as one of most versatile and ready of the patriotic poetic writers of the present day. Many brave comrades have been inspired and their loyal impulses quickened by the production of his pen. We have taken the liberty to reproduce one of his poems of special interest to those of the 121st.

Ingraham P. Smith, born at New Brunswick, Canada.

When six years old located at East Worcester. Attended common school and enlisted at Middlefield Aug. 8, 1862, in Co. G, 121st N. Y. V. During the mud march was taken with bilious fever and sent to Finley Hospital, Washington. The following May was put on special duty as guard at the hospital. September, 1863, sent to Convalescent camp near Alexandria. Was through the campaign in the Wilderness and wounded in the charge at Spotsylvania while on top of the rebel breast works, and sent to Armory Square hospital, Washington; thence to West Philadelphia hospital, granted fifteen day's furlough and returned to hospital. When Early threatened Washington, every man able to do garrison duty was ordered via. boat to Washington. Sent from here to distribution camp; on duty in the Quartermaster Department until Oct. 1, 1864. Rejoined his regiment at Cedar Creek. After his discharge he returned to Stratford, Fulton Co., and located at East Worcester in 1871. He engaged in the battles at Hampton Pass and in front of Petersburg before going to the hospital.

OFFICERS OF JOHNSON POST.

Harrison Pettie..	Commander.
Judson Goodenough,	Senior Vice-Commander.
Shas. W. Smith,	Junior Vice-Commander.
J. H. Goodrich,.	Adjutant.
Albert Foland,.	Quartermaster.
Perrin Waterman,	Chaplain.
	Surgeon.
Ransom Denoyles,	Officer of the Day.
James Kniskern,	Officer of the Guard.
A. D. Phillips,,	Quartermaster Sergeant.
J. K. Tyler,	Sergeant Major.

Past Commanders.

P. P. Bently,
W. L. Knapp,
Jay H. Goodrich,
Albert Foland,
Perrin Waterman,
Hiram Mereness,
Charles P. Childs,
S. M. Flint,
Frank McCormick.

List of Members.

Atkins, I. S., Steamer Malvern,	U. S. N.
Bentley, B. B.,	D, 3d N. Y. C.
Bentley, M. D.,	E, 1st N. Y. Eng.
Bert, John,	E, 1st N. Y. Eng.
Burnside, William,	Unknown.
Cain, George C.,	I, 51 N. Y.
Cepperly, David,	L, 3d N. Y. C.
Cheesbro, Ovid,	D, 3d N. Y. C.
Dutcher, W.,	F, 16 N. Y. H. A.
Dana, John K.,	D, 3d N. Y. C.
Diefendorf, Parmer,	L, 3d N. Y. C.
Denoyles, Ransom,	5th N. Y. Ind. Bat.
Freeman, James,	F, 177 N. Y.
Flint, S. M.,	H, 5th U. S. Cav.
Foland, A.,	H, 76, C, 147 N. Y.
Fisk, Fred W.,	8th N. Y. Bat.
Goodrich, Jay,	I, 121 N. Y.
Goodenough, Judson,	B, 92 N. Y.
Groat, John H.,	C, 3d N. Y. C.
Hughes, Sylvester,	3d N. Y. C.
Hallock, Alpheus,	Unknown.
Jaycox, Adelbert,	I, 121 N. Y.
Kniskern, James,	Unknown.
Knapp, W. L.,	D, 3d N. Y. C.
Lovejoy, John,	D, 10 N. Y. H. A.
Lovejoy, Allen,	G, 121 N. Y.
Leonard, W. H.,	I, 51 N. Y.
Mann, Geo. S.,	G, 124 N. Y.
Mallery, W. H.,	E, 1st N. Y. Eng.

McCormick, Frank, ...I, 152 N. Y.
Manning, Richard, ...Unknown.
Putman, Elijah, ...U. S. Navy.
Pitcher, Tobias, ...L, 3d N. Y. C.
Pettie, Harrison, ...K, 76 N. Y.
Phillips, A. D., ...F, 152 N. Y.
Rowell, G. W., ...G, 141 Ill.
Robinson, James W., ...B. 7th N. Y. S. G.
Sellew, George, ...C, 7th Conn.
Smith, Jerry, ...I, 51 N. Y.
Smith, I. P., ...G, 121 N. Y.
Strait, Peter J. ....C, 44 N. Y.
Sullivan, David E., ...I, 152 N. Y.
Spurbeck, Orlando, ...G, 134 N. Y.
Smith, D. S., ...H, 144 N. Y.
Stimpson, James, ...Unknown.
Tyler, J. K., ...G, 121 N. Y.
Timbrook, William, ...C, 144 N. Y.
Timbrook, Jerry, ...B, 2d N. Y. C.
Tripp, Perry, ...D, 17 Pa. Cav.
Weyman, Bennett, ...B, 101 N. Y.
Waterman, C. O. ....5th N. Y. Ind. Bat.
Waterman, Edwin R., ...3d N. Y. L. A.
Waterman, Perrin, ...G. 121 N. Y.
Wright, Geo. B., ...G, 48 Wis.
Wilsey, Chas. ....G, 121 N. Y.

In Memoriam.

Childs, C. P. .... I, 51 N. Y.
Sullivan, Wheeler, ... D, 152 N. Y.

Graves Decorated by Johnson Post, No. 25.

WAR OF 1861—1865.

Agan, Micheal P.
Bates, Wm.
Bruce, Wm.
Childs, Chas. P.
Esmay, Jerome.
Griggs, Wm.
Houghton, Clinton,
Jackson, Wm.
McLaughlen, Gen. N. B.
Monroe, Alfred,
Nizbeth, Tunis,
Pearsons, Wm. H.
Queal, Wm. S.
Sullivan, Wheeler.
Tabor, John,
Wright, Edgar K.
Wieting, John C., Jr.
Borne, Guilford,
Brown, Ezra,
Bushnell, David P.
Cushing, Chas. H.
Fields, Randolph.
Grant, Seth H.
Hartwell, Richard I.
Knapp, George H.
Markham, G. H.
Morehouse, Joseph.
Pearsons, Irving M.
Queal, Capt. Paul A.
Smith, Morton D.
Sullivan, John L.
Waterman, Silas.
Wright, Lieut. Orange,
Wilson, Simon,

MEXICAN WAR.

Capt. Leslie Chase.

WAR OF 1812.

Biglow, Cyrus,
Caryl, John,
Davis, Lorane.
Griswold, Wickham,
Childs, Samuel,
Crippen, Philip,
Dickenson, Wm.
Harington, Jacob H.

Race, Benjamin,   Williams, William,
Waterman, Roswell,   Wright, Orange,

REVOLUTION, 1776.

Dickenson, Seth,   Dickenson, Francis.
Davis, Joseph,   Green, Silas,
Hartwell, Solomon,   Hartwell, Samuel,
Queal, William M.   Stevens, Henry,
Waterman, John

TRIBUTE TO THE "ONESTERS."

BY JOHN K. TYLER.

When men sought the life of our nation
   And Rebels their work had begun
There formed on the banks of the Mohawk
   That Regiment—"One twenty one."
There were men of all trades and professions,
   There were "Big Joe" and Tim Dacy, too;
The people all cheered and they shouted
   When the boys marched away in their blue.

Brave men to the front were now rushing
   As streams going out from the fountain,
And in one short month we received
   Our baptismal fire at South Mountain.
Although we were not schooled as soldiers,
   We never had learned how to run;
And ours was a record of glory
   When led by brave Col. Upton.

The story of valor is written,—
 How they marched, how they fought and they bled;
How few there came back without blemish,
 And the many they left with the dead.
From South Mountain to old Appomatox
 Our battles were more than a score;
And they said when we passed in review,—
 "There's the pride of the fighting 6th Corps."

Right well we remember the ladies
 Who gave us the banner in trust,
And asked that we ever would guard it,
 And not see it trail in the dust.
And well we remember the welcome
 They gave our boys here in this town,
As rejoicing we came home from victory,
 When the last Rebel flag was torn down.

Here's health to the comrades from Otsego,
 And those from old Herkimer, too,
That stand here to-night reunited,
 Who fought for the red, white and blue.
Here's health to brave UPTON who led them
 No matter how strong were the foe,
Wherever the fight was the thickest
 There he and the "Onesters" would go

The memory of comrades we cherish,
 Whose faces are absent to-night.
Who fought for our Cause and the Union
 And fearlessly died for the right.
All honor to brothers and sisters,
 Who stood by the brave and the true,
Our flag and our country forever—
 Three cheers for the RED, WHITE and BLUE!

C. A. Shepherd Post, No. 189,

OTEGO, N. Y.

Regular meetings every Saturday evening at the G. A. R. Rooms.

THIS Post was organized, its charter received and mustered in to the department of New York, Dec. 29, 1880, by mustering officer, L. Coe Young, of Binghamton, N. Y., assisted by Comrade W. L. Curtis, of C. C. Siver Post, and other members from the Unadilla and Franklin Posts.

The Post was named in honor of and to perpetuate the name of a favored son and brave soldier enlisting from Otego, in the person of C. A. Shepherd.

T. H. Briggs was chosen first commander. He was born March 21, 1828, at Hartwick, Otsego Co., N. Y. Moved to Otego and attended the district schools, after leaving school learned the carpenter's trade. Enlisted at Oneonta, N. Y., Aug. 11, 1862, as a private in Co. K, 121st N.Y.V. and was mustered into the service at Camp Schuyler, Mohawk, N. Y., Aug. 23, 1862, Ordered to Washington and thence to the second battle of Fredericksburg, the 121st supporting battery May 3, 1863, while the light Division was charging, etc., capturing Mayre Heights on the same morning, and in the afternoon of the same day, engaged in the battle at Salem Church with the 6th Corps. The 121st lost at the battle in killed and wounded 273

R. C. HUNT,

Main St., - Otego, N. Y.

Dealer in

Dry Goods, Choice Groceries,

Ready-Made Pants in Wool and Cotton.

Hats, Caps, Boots and Shoes.

Underwear, Hosery and Notions

And articles usually found in a

First-Class Store.

Reasonable Rates.   Livery Attached.

CHARLES DAVIS,

Proprietor of

Empire House,

Gilbertsville, N. Y.

Favorite Resort for

Commercial Men & Summer Boarders.

Good Accommodations.   A Good Bar.

men. Going from here to Gettysburg, after battle followed Lee through Emmitsburg, Md., to Funkstown. At Rappahannock Station, Nov. 7, 1863, captured the rebel works and a large number of prisoners, and finishing the year's work on the Mine Run expedition, going into winter quarters at Hazel Run, near Brandy Station. The campaign of 1864 opens at the battle of the Wilderness, May 5 and 6. The 121st was one of the twelve picked regiments selected by and under command of Col. Upton to charge upon the enemy's works. Was wounded during this charge. (one of the grandest during the war) May 10, 1864, and sent to Harwood Hospital, Washington, D. C.; transferred to Camden, U. S. General Hospital, at Baltimore, where he remained until Sept. 11, 1864, sent to McClellan Hospital, Philadelphia, February, 1865, and remained here until he joined regiment in front of Petersburg, Feb. 22, 1865. Breaking of the lines in front of Petersburg on April 2, the 3rd Regiment of 2nd Division was sent to support the 9th Corps, in the works that they had captured, remained in the works until near daylight, the 121st N. Y. went over the works and received orders to deploy as skirmishers going to Petersburg or uniil they met the enemy, on the way captured two Forts with guns but no men. After passing the Forts the regiment reformed and marched into Petersburg before sun rise. Engaged in the battle of Sailor Creek April 6, 1865. Lee surrendering returned to Bakersville; thence with the 6th Corps to Danville, N. C. Regiment returned to Bakersville by rail, and was mustered out at Hall's Hill June 25, 1865. Briggs returning to Oneonta and in 1870 moved to Otego. Was a charter member of Shepherd Post, No. 189. Elected first commander for 1881 and again elected to serve during the year 1883. He displayed more than an ordinary amount of executive ability, and his administration was one of thorough disciplin and

C. E. MORRELL,

—DEALER IN—

Heavy & Shelf Hardware,

Stoves

AND

Ranges.

Repairing at Short Notice.

OUR PRICE IS LOW

—AND—

Guaranteed.

MAIN ST.,

OTEGO, · N. Y.

Otego Machine Shop.

GEO. L. STARR, Prop.

→ All Kinds of Machine Repairing. ←

Plumbing and Steam Fitting, Steel Stamps and Stencel plates, Types and Dyes for Cutting Threads, &c.

COR. OF FOLLET AND CENTRE STS.,   OTEGO, N.Y.

resulted in substantial benefit to the post. He was again chosen commander to serve during the present year—1892. He is now residing on Main St., Otego, N. Y., and is in the employ of the Bowe Casket Company.

Wm. H. Baldwin, commander of post during the year 1885, was born in Otego in 1838, educated at the common schools and learned the blacksmith trade. He enlisted Nov. 1, 1861, as a private in Co. C, 76 Reg. N. Y. V. (Enrolling in the Otsego branch at Cherry Valley as a member of the 39th Reg., but at Albany was consolidated with 76th Reg.) Going from Albany to New York to Park Barracks, thence to Riker Island and Washington to Merredian Hill; thence to Fort Stevens and Fredericksburg, to re-enforce Pope at Cedar mountain, fell back and engaged all the way to Bull Run during Pope's retreat. Engaged in 2nd Bull Run and Gain's Hill, returned to Arlington Heights, engaging in the battle at South Mountain Sept. 14, 1861, then through Washington to the battle of Antietam Sept. 17, remained here four weeks, engaged in battle at Snecker's Gap Nov. 1 to 3. Ordered back and engaged in battle of Fredericksburg Dec. 12 and 13, 1862. Went into camp at Pratt's Point and ordered out to join Burnside during his famous Mud March, then back to camp for winter quarters. In spring of 1863 participated in the battle of Chancellorsville, Va., from May 1 to 5, Gettysburg July 1 to 4, Mine Run Nov. 27, 1863, and at the battle of the Wilderness May 5 and 6. Was with three companys taken prisoners while on the skirmish line and sent to Andersonville, thence to Florence, S. C., and paroled by special exchange of sick and wounded and sent to Annapolis, Md., to Parole Camp, and granted a thirty day's furlough. In February, 1865, reported at Annapolis, his term of enlistment having expired Nov. 1, 1864. He was sent to Albany and learned

TOBEY & GURNEYS.

The extensive establishment of this firm is deserving of special mention, it being one of the most spacious and elegant Dry Goods and Carpet emporiums in Otsego Co., occupying a central position on Main St. and extending a wide influence over the trade in the county, their sales rooms being the largest in Oneonta. occupying three floors 24 x 100, and a basement of the same size for surplus stock. The first floor is devoted to the Dry Goods department where everything in the line of Foreign and Domestic Dry Goods, Ladies Furnishing Goods of the very best grades, makes and styles can be found in endless variety, including fine Silks and Dress Goods in the latest styles and novelties The second floor is given to Carpets, Draperies Cloaks, etc. In every department of trade among the many successful houses, in the various lines of commercial enterprise, some one will stand out conspicuously as a leader in each especial branch In the Carpet trade of this section Tobey & Gurneys stand preeminent. It would be impossible, within the limit of this brief sketch, to describe even a portion of the magnificent stock carried in this department. The owners of the finest houses in Oneonta, have, after visiting this room, purchased Carpets, Curtains and Draperies from this firm. Everything new, tasteful and useful in Carpets, Draperies, Oil Cloth, Mattings, Antique Rugs and Upholstery can be found in great variety, quality, quantity and price. In Ladies' and Misses Wraps, only a visit to the department will convey an idea of the great variety on exhibition. The third floor is used for the making of carpets, where many hands are kept busy making carpets for their extensive trade. The individual members of the firm are A. B. Tobey, M. Gurney and E. G. Gurney. The business is a continuation of that which was established in January, 1867, by H. M. Tobey & Sons the junior of the latter firm being the Mr. Tobey of the present firm. Mr. M. Gurney entered the house in 1873 and Mr. E. J. Gurney in 1883 when the firm name became as at present. Eight polite and attentive clerks are employed in the different departments and their trade, unsurpassed by any similar house in the county, is made up of the best and most fashionable people in the community.

there that they had no description list. He was sent home again and in three weeks, becoming quite anxious for his discharge, made another visit to Albany, with the same results. He procured transportation to Washington in March, and from here to his regiment, remained until after the surrender of Lee, he was discharged May 26, 1865, returned to Otego and resumed blacksmithing. He was a brave soldier and did splendid service on the march and in the field. Is a charter member of Shepherd Post served for four terms as Senior Vice Commander, three terms Officer of the Day and elected Commander one year and is at the present time Senior Vice Commander.

S. S. Sheldon, born in the town of Otego, N. Y., March 9, 1838, educated at the district school and worked at the carpenter and joiners trade until the war broke out. He enlisted Aug. 6, 1862, in Co. K, 121st N. Y. V. Mustered in at Camp Schuyler, Mohawk, Aug. 25, 1862, under Capt. S. M. Olin. Ordered to the Army of the Potomac, 2nd Brigade 6th Corps 1st Division, remained in Washington a few days and joined the army of South Mountain. Participated in the battles of Fredericksburg and severely wounded by bullet in the left side at the battle of Salem Church May 3, 1862 and sent to Carver Hospital, Washington, remained six months discharged and joined his regiment near Charleston, Va., engaged in the battles in which this regiment fought until the war closed and discharged at Hall's Hill June 25, 1865. He enlisted as a private and after muster was promoted to Corporal and acted as Comissary Sergeant for the company until discharged, was promoted to Sergeant for bravery on the battle field. Returned to Otego in 1875 and joined Shepherd Post as charter member and elected Junior Vice Commander at the first meeting. Served as Senior Vice Commander and three years Quartermaster, and elected Commander to serve during the year 1891, and is now

E. B. RATHBUN,

—DEALER IN—

Groceries and Family Supplies,

Dress Goods, Fancy Goods,
Boots, Shoes, Hats,
Caps, &c.,
Main St., OTEGO, N.Y.

J. Henry Castle,

DEALER IN

General * Merchandise.

ALL KINDS OF

FARM ✦ MACHINERY,

AND

BLACKSMITH and WAGON MAKER,

AGENT FOR THE

Champion Mowing Machine,

LOCATED ON

FLAX ISLAND CREEK, - OTEGO, N. Y.

FARM PRODUCE BOUGHT AND SOLD.

serving his first year as Justice of the Peace for the third term.

Ward Olney Card was born April 30, 1830, near Elizabeth, Otsego Co., N. Y., his parents locating in Morris when he was a little more than a year old. He attended the district schools, and when 16 years old went to work in a cotton factory at Morris, where he remained for two years. He then learned the carriage making trade. In 1862 he moved to Cooperstown, where he worked at the carpenter trade until he enlisted, Dec. 31, 1863, as a private in the 16th N. Y., H. A., Co. A. Was mustered at Norwich and ordered to Fort Schuyler, near New York, thence to Glouchester Point, off Yorktown, remaining here until August, when he was sent to Bermuda Front. The regiment was detailed here to dig Butler's Dutch Gap Canal; next going to front of Petersburg, where they remained until Oct. 1st, and crossed over to the North side of the James River and made a raid toward Richmond; next engaging in the battle of Chapin's Farm, and after the fight established a line of defense, remaining in this position until they were ordered to Fort Fisher under Gen. Terry, and participating in its capture. After the battle of Fort Fisher the command came North with prisoners to Elmira, and were then ordered to report at Fort Caswell, ten miles up the coast from Fort Fisher. July 16 was ordered to Baltimore and to Washington, to Forts North and Williams on the Heights between Washington and Alexandria. Aug. 20, ordered to Hearts Island, and discharged Aug. 28, '65. Returned to Otego, joined Kidder Post at Morris soon after, and taking a transfer card, joined Shepherd Post No. 189. He is now residing on Main street, Otego, N. Y., with his daughter, Mrs. E. W. Bates.

OTEGO VARIETY STORE.

MAIN ST., - - OTEGO, N. Y.

One of the most progressive business houses in Otego is that of the above named store, one of the oldest in Otsego Co., being established in the year 1822. Mr. Annable first entered the store in 1879 as a clerk, and became a member of the firm of Annable & Russell in 1882, and on Jan 1, 1892, purchased Mr. Russell's interest, thereby becoming sole proprietor. Here everything usually kept in a *first-class* general merchandise store can be found, occupying three floors and basement. The salesroom is on the main floor where you can find all the latest styles of Dry Goods, Fancy Goods, Notions, Hats and Caps, Gents' Furnishing Goods, Jewelry, and a full line of choice Groceries, Canned Goods, &c. The floor adjoining is used for heavy groceries. The second floor is devoted to Wall Paper, Curtains, Carpets and Oil Cloths in quality, styles and prices to suit all customers The basement is used for storing surplus stock. The storehouse, consisting of two floors, is just back of the store. This building is well stocked with Salt and Dried Meats, Rubber Goods, Flour, Salt, Tobacco, &c. Mr. Annable, always caring for the numerous wants of his patrons, is assisted by polite and attentive clerks under his personal supervision. A gentleman of pronounced business ability, courteous manners, and strict integrity have gained for him a host of friends throughout this section and enabled him to build up the handsome trade he now enjoys.

Hiram Baldwin was born in the town of Meredith, Delaware Co., April 8th, 1834, locating with his parents at Otego in 1835, receiving his education at the common schools. After leaving school, he learned the blacksmith trade, and enlisted in Aug. 1864, as private in the 144th Regiment, N. Y. V., but was mustered into the 1st N. Y. Eng. at Norwich, N. Y. Going to New York, and thence to Hearts Island to City Point, and from here to Alexandria, to Hilton Head, arriving at that place Oct. 1st. In December, went to Tillifamy, engaging in battle there; thence to Port Royal Ferry, and laid pontoon bridge for one wing of Sherman's Army on his march from Savannah to Charleston, S. C. Went from here to Savannah, Ga., then to Hilton Head, and was discharged in July, 1865. Returned to Otego, was a charter member of Shepherd Post 189, and has held the office of Senior Vice, Chaplain, Adjutant and Quartermaster. Has served as Overseer of the Poor for the town of Otego. He is now residing on Follet street with his family; has one son, aged 26, residing at Atalanta, Ga., a daughter, Mrs. W. H. Barry, residing at Otego, and another daughter now residing at Binghamton, N. Y.

Andrew J. Reymore was born at Franklin, March 30, 1838; enlisted in Aug. 1862, as private in Co. B., 44th N. Y. V.; was taken sick with fever and sent to the hospital in Oct., 1862. He remained six months, was sent to the convalescent camp and discharged for general disability.

Walter Whitney was born at Sidney, Delaware Co. N. Y., on the 22nd day of August, 1828, and was educated at the common school at Sidney. He enlisted Sept. 12, 1864, at Otego, N. Y., in Co. B., 90th Reg., N. Y. V. He served with his regiment on the weary march and on the field with undaunted courage and devotion to duty, until he

SUSQUEHANNA HOTEL,

J. T. TOMPKINS, Prop'r.

Main St., - - Otego, N. Y.

=== FIRST CLASS IN EVERY RESPECT. ===

Headquarters for Commercial Men

PROF. GEO. H. FANCHER,

(Graduate of the German Composer, E. Zimmermann.)

Piano and Organ Instructor,

— TEACHER OF —

Vocal and Instrumental Music,

Thorough-base and Harmony,

AND DEALER IN ALL KINDS OF

MUSICAL INSTRUMENTS.

UNADILLA, - - - N. Y.

was discharged June 3, 1865. He is now residing at Shepherd Corners, Otego, with his family, and is at the present time Deputy Sheriff of Otsego county. He is an active member of Shepherd Post No. 189.

J. T. Tompkins was born at Maryland, Otego Co., N. Y., Dec. 16, 1836. and was educated at the common schools of that place. After leaving school he learned the mason trade. He enlisted Aug. 23, 1861. as a private in Co. D., 3rd N. Y. Cavalry. He was a born soldier, always at his post of duty, and served with great fidelity, participating in all the marches, skirmishes, and engagements of his regiment, until they were discharged at Suffolk. Va., June 7th, 1865. After his discharge he returned to Maryland and worked at his trade. He was a charter member of Brown Post No. 25, organized at Schenevus in 1874. He remained at Maryland until April 1, 1889, when he moved to Otego and became the proprietor of the Susquehanna House. where he is now residing with his family, consisting of an estimable wife and son, W. H., aged 25 years. This hotel, under his management, is one of the best between Albany and Binghamton.

Soloman N Goodrich. born at Davenport, Delaware Co., N. Y , April 19, 1823, attended the District schools, moved to Harpersfield, and and in 1840 located at Oneonta, N. Y. Went from Oneonta to Harmony, Susquehanna county, Pa.. and back to Otego, going on a farm. He enlisted in Sept., 1862, as a private in Co. G, 152 N. Y. V. Mustered into the U. S. service at Camp Schuyler, Mohawk, N. Y., and ordered to Chain Bridge—to the defence of Washington. Remained here until April, 1863, and ordered to Suffolk, in the dismal swamp. The regiment had received orders and had started for Gettysburg, during the raid into Pennslvania, but was ordered back

L. G. WARNER,

Successor to Park & Ward,

MANUFACTURER OF

Fine Monumental Work

AND DEALER IN THE BEST GRADES OF

New England and Foreign Granites

AT LOWEST PRICES,

GILBERTSVILLE, N. Y.

Special attention to Soldier's Monuments and work ordered by Posts. Graves of Indigent Soldiers marked as far as possible without cost.

KEYSTONE ✸ HOUSE,

M. M. BISHOP, Prop.,

MORRIS, = N. Y.

First-Class in Every Respect.

The table, under the personal supervision of Mrs. Bishop, contains all the delacacies of the season.

Fine Sample Room. :-: Good Bar.

Accommodation for Both Man and Beast.

to guard stores, and returned to Washington, remained here but three days, when they were ordered to New York to the riot; remained in New York until Oct., when they received orders to go to Washington. Was sent from here to Convalescent Camp, in three weeks after was assigned to the Invalid Corps, 1st Company. Did guard duty in Washington until discharged Dec. 23, 1864. Returned to Otego, joined Shepherd Post and is at the present time Surgeon of the Post. He is now residing with his wife on Main street, Otego, N. Y.

Franklin Allen, born in the town of Bristol, Hartford Co., Conn., March 2, 1822. Moved with his parents, when 7 years old, to Meredith, Delaware Co., N. Y., and attended the common school. In 1852 removed to Otego, remained three years, returned to Meredith, and in 1862 moved to Otego and enlisted Sept. 3, '62, as a private in Co. G, 152 Regt. N. Y. V., was mustered at Camp Schuyler, under Col. Boyer, was sent to Judiciary Square Hospital, Washington, remaining there three months. The record of the regiment is his record. Discharged April 8, 1864. Returned to Otego, and joined Post in 1885. He is now residing with his wife on River street, Otego, N. Y.

Edgar Redington, an active member, and at the present time Officer of the Day, enlisted in Co. C, 114th N. Y. V. He was a model soldier, serving with his regiment, and engaging in all its marches, skirmishes, and participating in every action in which they were engaged. There were many brave men in the 114th N. Y. V., but there were none more faithful in the performance of their duty than Edgar Redington. He was always at his post, and of a genial disposition, always looking at the bright side of life in camp, and making dark hours bright. There are

J. CEPERLEY,

Blacksmtthing and Iron Work

IN ALL ITS BRANCHES.

Special Attention Given to Wood Work and Wagon Rapairing.

OTEGO, N. Y,

J. R. THORPE,

Gen'l Insurance and Real Estate Ag't

MAIN ST., OTEGO, N. Y.

☞ Those having property to sell or rent, or wishing to buy, should consult Mr. Thorpe. Correspondence solicited.

W. J. SIMMONS,

Boot, Shoe and Harness Maker,

RIVER ST., - OTEGO, N. Y.

First-Class Work.   Prices Guaranteed.

✸ REPAIRING NEATLY AND PROMPTLY DONE. ✸

many comrades who will recall with pleasure many incidents in camp, not on the programme of the monotonous details of camp life, where Comrade Redington was the leading spirit. He is an active member of the Post and always taking a deep interest in its welfare.

T. L. Hunt was born in the town of Otego, Nov. 26. 1839, and was educated at the common schools. He enlisted at Fairbury, Ill., Aug. 29, 1862, as a private in Co. E, 129th Reg., Ill. Vols. He served with his regiment on the march and in the field, and for distinguished service and good conduct was promoted to sergeant. Discharged June 8. 1865, locating at Otego, he joined Shepherd Post No. 189. He is at the present time the Quartermaster of the Post, residing in the village of Otego, and employed at the Bowe Casket Co.

James H. Whitney was born at Sidney, Delaware Co.. N. Y., Aug. 29, 1842, attending the district school at that place. He enlisted from the town of Otego, N. Y., in Oct. 1861, as a private in Co. K., 76th Regt. N. Y. V. Was mustered into the U. S. service at Albany. Going to the front via New York, was sent to the hospital in Jany. '62, and discharged in March 1862. He joined Shepherd Post as a charter member, and moving to Clinton, Oneida Co., N. Y., taking a transfer card, joined the Hinkley Post. He returned to Otego in 1887, is now residing on Main street, and is employed at the Bowe Casket works.

Darius Henderson was born in the town of Schoharie. Schoharie Co., N. Y., Aug. 10, 1815, going with his parents in 1817 to Walton, Delaware Co., where he was educated at the common schools. Leaving school, he embarked in the wool carding and cloth dressing business.

COTTAGE HOTEL,

WELLS BRIDGE, N. Y.,

C. J. COLLINS, - - PROPRIETOR.

Reasonable Rates by Day or Week.

Sample Room for Commercial Men.

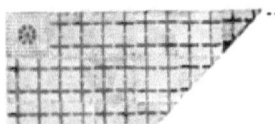

F. C. ADAMS,
DEALER IN
WATCHES, CLOCKS, JEWELRY, DIAMONDS,
MUSICAL INSTRUMENTS, &c.
Repairing in all its Branches Promptly Executed.
Main Street, OTEGO, N. Y.

TILLEY BLAKELY,
ATTORNEY AND COUNCELLOR AT LAW
PENSION AND CLAIM AGENT,
OFFICE: BOWE BLOCK,
MAIN STREET, OTEGO, N. Y.
NOTARY PUBLIC.

Locating at Mt. Upton, in company with Erastus Rockwell, was engaged in the manufacture of cloth, remaining here during the years 1852-'53. Located at Otego in 1854. purchasing a farm of seventy.five acres, and engaged in farming and the lumber business, but still giving part of his time to wool-carding, his former business. He moved in 1858 to Walton, Delaware Co., and enlisted Aug. 18, 1862, as a private in Co. B., 144th Reg., N. Y. V. Was mustered into the U. S. service at Elmira, N. Y., on the 22nd day of Sept., 1862, going to Camp Bliss, Upton Hill, and Cloud Mills in defence of the Capitol. Was sick. and sent to hospital at Washington, and detailed as Company cook: soon after was detailed by the surgeon. Dr. Leal, as hospital cook director, in charge of cooking and the preparation of food for sick soldiers. Was discharged January, 1863, and returned to Walton. Moved to Spencer, Tioga Co., N. Y, in 1866, taking up his residence in Troy, Pa., in 1879, he remained here until 1881. Moved to Franklin, residing here until 1885, when he returned to Otego, While at Troy, Pa., he joined the Gustin Post. and became a member of the Shepherd Post by transfer card in 1885, and has served as Chaplain of the Post. Was Justice of the Peace at Spencer for eight years, and Collector of the town of Otego for two years. He is now, (with an estimable wife,) residing on Main street, Otego. N. Y. His son, Vernon F., aged 23, a brave soldier, enlisted in the 6th Pennsylvania Reserves, Co. K., and was kiled at the battle of Fredericksburg, Dec. 13, 1862, was buried on the field and now fills an unknown grave. Jennie was married to Chas. Cowell of Newark, N. J.; went to Florida in 1885, and died aged 49. Alice Irena, wife of Rev. C. M. Jones, District Missionary in the Baptist denomination, is now residing at Oneonta, N. Y., and Carrie E., wife of Fred B. Lewis, is now residing at West Danby, Tompkins county, N. Y.

E. D. MOORE,

Corner Store, GILBERTSVILLE, N. Y.

Clothing & Gent's Furnishing Goods.

Hats, Caps, Boots, Shoes,

UMBRELLAS, NOTIONS, &c.

AGENT FOR

The Celebrated Silver and Gold Shirts.

PROF. M. H. ELDERKIN,

OF THE

❀ NEW ENGLAND CONSERVATORY OF MUSIC, BOSTON, ❀

TEACHER OF

PIANO, ORGAN, VIOLIN, GUITAR, VOICE CULTURE AND MUSICAL COMPOSITION.

Tuning and regulating of the highest order. Organ tuning a specialty. Certified exponent of the renowned Petersilea System, the most severely classical method ever compiled for the piano. Thirty years experience on the piano.

BINGHAMTON, - - N. Y.

The history of the Post would be incomplete did we fail to mention Mr. R. R. Guernsey, now doing business at Newark, N. J. Mr. Guernsey enlisted as a member of Company M, 3d N. Y. L. A., and served faithfully and conscientiously throughout, participating in numerous battles, campaigns, &c. He was a cool and intrepid fighter, and most companiable gentleman. His dignity and scholarly attainments have made for him many friends. He is of a quiet and reserved disposition, though a genial companion, prompt in his dealing, and (although not set in his ways) has a strict regard for that which he thinks is right. He was a prominent and active member of the Post, and from his known experience and wisdom, important matters coming before the Post receive the benefit of his counsel and advice.

John Lunn, now residing in Otsdawa, is numbered among the brave men, who in the hour of his country's greatest need, left friends and the pleasures of home to share the pain and privations of a soldier's life,—to battle for the right. He enlisted in Co. C., 2nd Minn. Cavalry, and did splendid service in the field, serving with undaunted courage and devotion to duty. He is an active member of Shepherd Post 189, and a true friend and respected citizen.

James Craft, now residing in Oneonta, is an honored member of Shepherd Post. He enlisted in Co. A. 1st Penn. Light Artillery, serving with his battery, enduring its hardships and making many sacrifices, that his country, which he loved so well, might live. Although not able to meet regularly with the comrades of the Shepherd Post, he still retains a lively interest in all that pertains to the welfare of the Post and the comrades connected therewith.

Adelbert Hughston was born in the town of Otego, Dec. 29, 1842, educated at the common schools, and learned the coopers trade. He enlisted from New Lisbon, Aug. 1864, and was mustered into the U. S. service at Norwich, as a recruit for Co. C., 3rd N. Y. C. Going to the front at once, to City Point, he joined his regiment in Kautz' Div. 2nd Brigade, engaging in the battle at Prince George Court House, Sept. 28, and Johnson's Farm Oct 7th, '64. On the 7th of October, a large body of the enemy's infantry, under the command of Gen. Lee in person, made an attack on Kautz's division at "Johnson's Farm," on the Darbytown road, north of the James, and within 7 miles from Richmond. Col. Jacobs in his report said, "The engagement was the fiercest, most sanguinary and destructive of all in which the cavalry had taken a prominent part during the year. The division was finally driven back at the point of the bayonet, the 3rd, under Colonel Jacobs, being the last regiment to leave the field. To show the desperate nature of the contest, it may be stated that of the 3rd, more than half, and of the staff of the 2nd Brigade, to which the 3rd was attached, all of the officers, (five in number) except Col. West, commanding, were either killed or wounded." He also participated in Butler's cattle raid, when Longstreet stole 225 head of cattle from Butler. Oct. 10th, '64, was sent with some others to Brigade headquarters, Col. West, commanding. Was thrown from his horse and injured, and was sent to Point of Rocks hospital, remained two weeks, sent home on furlough; rejoined his regiment at Reams Station, did picket duty on the North Carolina line until the evacuation of Richmond; sent on raid to Edmiston, N. C., which resulted in the rebels becoming short of many horses, mules, chickens and a large amount of bacon, together with several barrels of apple jack. Returned to old quarters at Great Bridge, N. C. June 1, 1865, was ordered to report to Suffolk, where they were discharged June 7,'65. Returned to Otego and joined Shepherd Post as a charter member, serving three years as Commander, two years as Quartermaster and is now serving his fourth year as Adjutant. His administration as Commander resulted in a substantial benefit to the Post. He is now residing on Main street, Otego, N. Y.

OFFICERS OF SHEPHERD POST.

T. H. Briggs, ...Commander.
William Baldwin,..............Senior Vice-Commander.
Darius Henderson,.............Junior Vice-Commander.
A. E. Hughston, ... Adjutant.
T. L Hunt,....................Quartermaster.
Solomon Goodrich,............Surgeon.
Hiram Baldwin,...............Chaplain.
Edgar Redington,........ ....Officer of the Day.
S S. Sheldon,...................Officer of the Guard.

PAST COMMANDERS.

T. H. Briggs,   A. H. Hunt,   L. M. Stanton,
Wm. Baldwin,   A. E. Hughston, S. S. Sheldon

LIST OF MEMBERS.

Allen, Franklin............ ....G, 152, N. Y.
Burrell, A P..B, 4 Mich.
Briggs, T. H...K, 121, N. Y.
Baldwin, William H.... ....K, 76, N. Y
Baldwin, Hiram.....................................A, 1st N. Y. Eng.
Borden, Eugene............................ ....B, 51, N. Y.
Baldwin, H. J........... . ...E, 7 N. Y H. A.
Craft, James...A, 1st Pa. L. A.
Card, Olney.. H. Art.

Coryell, Nathen, Col..................A. 89, N. Y.
Fowler, F. H.........................A, 15 Ill.
Goodrich Solomon....................G, 152 N. Y.
Gurnsey, R. R.......................M, 3 L. A.
Hughston, A. E......................G, 3 N. Y. C.
Hunt, A. H..........................K, 11 Wis. V.
Hunt, T. L..........................E, 129 Ill.
Henderson, D........................I, 144 N. Y.
Lamb, Henry.........................B, 90 N. Y.
Lunn, John..........................C, 2 Minn. Cav.
Rollins, Charles....................B, 4 Mich.
Redington, E........................C, 114 N. Y.
Reynolds, Jacob.....................A, 1st N. Y. Eng.
Stanton, L M........................D, 1st N. Y. Mtd R.
Sheldon, S. S.......................K, 121 N. Y.
Utter, Geo. V.......................A, 19 H. A.
Whitney, Walter.....................B, 90 N. Y.
Whitney, J. H.......................K, 76 N. Y.

In Memoriam.

Williams, John......................K, 121 N. Y.
Whitney, William....................G, 152 N. Y.
Burnside, Adelbert..................E, 36 Ill. V.

Graves Decorated by Shepuere Post, No. 189.

Banker, Thorn	Burnside, Adelbert
Bailey, Thomas	Chatfield Oscar

Crandall, Henry / Dart, Marshall
Fowler, Adelbert / French, Abel
Goodrich, Hiram / Greene, Solomon
McCall, Thomas J / Miller, Gilbert
Martin, Samuel / Shepherd, Chas A
Williams, Monroe / Williams, John
Whitney, William

WAR OF 1812.

Burdick, Ephriam / Northrup, John
Foote, Harmon / Phelps, Horace
French, ———— / Tracy Capt. Ezeikel
Hale, Levi / Youmans, John
Benjamin Edson, Rev War

CHARLES F. BLACKMAN,

Funeral Director and Furnisher,

And Practical Embalmer.

Graduate of United States College of Embalming, New York.
Prof. A. Renouard, Demonstrator.

AND DEALER IN

Parlor and Chamber Furniture,

FANCY ROCKERS,

SPRING BEDS AND MATTRESSES,

Gilbertsville, Otsego Co., N. Y.

WM. M. DEITZ,

PUBLISHER OF

The Otsego Journal,

— AND DEALER IN —

FINE STATIONERY, BOOKS, ETC.

GILBERTSVILLE, N. Y.

W. A. Musson Post, No. 223,
GILBERTSVILLE, N. Y.

Regular Meetings Second and Fourth Saturdays in each month at G. A. R. Hall

THE W. A. Musson Post was organized at Gilbertsville, in the town of Butternuts, in June, 1881. Charter was received and mustered into the department of New York, June 30, '81, by Gen'l. James T. Bartlett, of Watrous Post, Binghamton, N. Y., assisted by Comrades from that Post. J. G. Bloodgood was elected Commander. The Post was named in honor of a brave soldier and scholar, an honored and respected citizen, W. A. Musson, born in the town of Butternuts, three miles from Gilbertsville, attending the common schools, and completing his education at the Gilbertsville academy. Taught school for a short time, then going on a farm. In Oct. 1861 he joined the army, enlisting as a member of the Band connected with the 51st Regt. The War department issuing an order doing away with the Bands connected with the Army, he was discharged. Returned to Gilbertsville, and in three weeks after he re-enlisted as a private in Co. G, 52nd N. Y. V. Was mustered into the U. S. service and commissioned 2nd Lieutenant, at Camp Schuyler, and detailed as Adjutant of the regiment, in the absence of Adjutant Quaff. Was soon after promoted to First Lieutenant, and assigned to the command of Co. C., and at the battle of Bloody Angle, was wounded, but refused to go to the hospital. Engaging in the battle

A. L. CAMP,

MANUFACTURER OF

ALL KINDS OF HARNESS.

A GENERAL LINE OF

Horse Furnishing Goods,

Whips, Blankets and Fly Nets,

ALL KINDS OF REPAIRING PROMPTLY AND NEATLY DONE.

A large assortment of

Heavy and Light Harness,

Made up of No. 1 Stock at the Lowest Prices.

GILBERTSVILLE, Otsego County, N. Y.

Call and Examine my work.

A. L. SKUSE,

Carriage Making

AND REPAIRING,

Saw Guming & Filing,

—AGENT FOR—

NEW HOME

Sewing Machine,

MACHINE OIL AND NEEDLES FOR ALL MACHINES.

ALL KINDS OF SEWING MACHINES REPAIRED.

GILBERTSVILLE,............ ..OTSEGO CO. N. Y.

of the Wilderness, he was again wounded in the thigh and sent to the Seminary Hospital, Germanstown. Was granted a furlough and reached his home at Gilbertsville, July 2, 1864. For distinguished service in the Wilderness, he was promoted to Captain, receiving his commission while at his home, Aug. 19th, '64; rejoined his regiment, then in camp in front of Petersburg. He was in command of the regiment at Burgess Farm, the battle of Hatche's Run, Oct. 4, '64. Capt. Musson had ordered the regiment to lie down in the rear of the Wm. Burgess Mansion, he pacing the ground to and fro as a target for the enemy. Friday morning, by a flank movement, he took a position supporting a battery which was dealing out shot and shell across the valley, doing havoc in the rebel ranks. Capt. Musson walked a few paces from the regiment, reclined upon a hill-side watching the execution of our shells. He called for an officer to accompany him, when a return shot struck him, killing him instantly. He was a young man, brave and efficient in duty, and a good commander. The following October his father, in company with Lieut. Stebbins, sought his grave and procured his remains, which were taken to Gilbertsville, and in Nov. 1865, were buried in Brookside cemetery. He was of a genial disposition, a fine singer, a true friend and christian gentleman. " None knew him but to love him ; none named him but to praise."

> " In the God of battles trust,
> Die we may, and die we must ;
> But O, where can dust to dust
> Be consigned so well !"

T. H. Musson was born January 26, 1845, at Gilbertsville, N. Y., where he was educated at the common schools, and enlisted Dec.(1863, when only 17 years old, as a private in Co. E., 2nd N. Y. H. A. Was mustered into

CARRIAGE PAINTING.   ORNAMENTAL PAINTING.

O. C. ADAMS,
Painting and Paper Hanging,
GILBERTSVILLE, N. Y.

HOUSE PAINTING.   SIGN PAINTING.

H. D. Donaldson,
GILBERTSVILLE, N. Y.

DEALER IN

Drugs, Medicines Chemicals,
Fine Toilet Soaps,
Perfumery and Fancy Articles.
Trusses, Pure Wines and Liquors, Stationery,
Paints, Oils, Varnishes and Dye Stuffs.

Physicians' Prescriptions Carefully Compounded

the service at Norwich, N. Y., the same month, ordered to Elmira, and from here to his regiment at Washington, joining his company at Fort Bennett, where they had been assigned to duty. Remained here until the campaign of 1864. In May 1864, the regiment was ordered to take the field as Infantry. Was wounded at the battle of Coal Harbor June 4, 1864, the ball passing through his right side, and then through a comrade in the rear rank, the missle taking the same course, and wounding both men in the same place. The soldiers lay for some time, one on each side of the road, when they were separated. Nearly a quarter of a century had passed, when Musson received a call from the comrade who had fought in the same battle, was wounded by the same ball, in exactly the same place. After he was picked up, was sent to Howard Hospital at Washington, and transferred to McClellan Hospital, Philadelphia. Granted a furlough, he arrived at Gilbertsville July 17, and returned to hospital the same day, and to the field soon after. Was again wounded at the battle of Reams Station. Sec. of War Stanton issued a special order, permitting a substitute to be furnished for Musson, and he was brought home and has since resided in Gilbertsville, where he has an estimable wife, the sister of Col. Rockwell, who was at the death beds of both Presi-dent Lincoln and Garfield. He is a charter member of Musson Post, has served as Commander for three years, and is at the present writing Surgeon of the Post.

Rufus B. Myrack was born at Winfield, Herkimer Co., N. Y., where he attended the common schools until eight years old; then going to the Gilbertsville Academy for two years, and completing his education at the Colgate Academy at Hamilton, N. Y. In 1860 he went to Iowa, and taught school. While here he enlisted, Aug. 17, 1861, as a private in Co. I., 2nd Iowa Cav.; was mustered into

Leading the Trade—Standing High Above All Competition—We Find

W. F. WARD'S
GENERAL - MERCHANDISE - STORE

IS THE PLACE TO BUY

DRY GOODS,
GROCERIES,

BOOTS and SHOES,

Ladies' Patent Leather and English Red Ties,

Misses and Children's Ties,

TRUNKS, BAGS AND VALISES,

Hats, Gloves and Neckwear,

And a Choile Line of Family Supplies,

Gilbertsville, Otsego Co., N.Y.

the U. S. service at Davenport, Iowa, and sent to Benton Barracks, St. Louis; thence to Buds Point, to Fort Pillow and Harrison Landing, Tenn; then, after the battle of Shiloh to Corinth, after Price's evacuation; engaging in the battles of Farmington, Glendale, Boonville and Iuka, Miss.; at Corinth, Water Valley and Coffeeville in Oct., 1862. Went into winter quarters at La Grange, Tenn. In the spring and summer of 1863, did patrol duty and skirmishing between Memphis and Corinth, on the Memphis and Charleston railroad, participating in the battle of Colliersville, Tenn. He was assigned to duty as Issuing Clerk, head-quarters of the Cavalry corps at Memphis, where he remained until Feb'y., 1864. Re-enlisted while here in the same company and regiment, and was granted a thirty day's furlough. At the expiration of same, he returned to his regiment at Davenport, Iowa; was ordered to Memphis and to Colliersville, thence to Germantown and White Station. When the three year's men left the regiment, he started on a sixty day's trip to Nashville, engaging in battle at Shoal Creek and Nashville, Tenn. Jan. 15, 1865. Was detailed as Regimental clerk at Colliersville, but remained with his regiment until the battle of Nashville. Rejoined regiment at Gravelly Springs, going from here to Harrisburg Landing, Tenn., thence to Iuka. Lee surrendering, he was sent to Decatur, Alabama. Detailed as Brigade Quartermaster's clerk, and left at Decatur in charge of unserviceable Quartermaster stores. Discharged Oct. 4, 1865, at Davenport, Iowa. Going to Gilbertsville, Nov. 7, '65, he joined the Musson Post as a charter member, and elected Quartermaster, serving until he was elected Commander for the year 1883. He is now residing with his family,—a wife and daughter aged 15—at Gilbertsville, N. Y., one son, aged 23, residing in New York. He enlisted as a private, and was for bravery promoted to sergeant. Has served as

Adjutant, Officer of the Day, and is at the present time Quartermaster-Sergeant.

Andrew J. Cowan was born in Scotland, in 1839, coming to America and locating at Albany, N. Y., in 1849; attended the common schools for nearly two years, then going to New York, went to school until 16 years old. Moved to Butternuts, Otsego Co., in 1855, and enlisted at Gilbertsville as a private in Co. K., 121st Reg. N. Y. V., Aug. 13th, 1862. Was wounded at the battle of Fredericksburg, May 3rd, '63, and sent to Carver hospital at Washington, March 1st, 1863. Soon after was sent to Convalescent camp, was here examined and sent back to Washington to Camp Depot, and assigned to the 75th Co. 2nd Batallion, stationed at Washington. Remained there until mustered out by General Order of the War Department No. 116, July 1, 1865. Was charter member of Musson Post; served as Senior-Vice, Quartermaster, and elected Commander to succeed Comrade R. B. Myrick, and is at present Adjutant of the Post, enlisting as a private, but was promoted for bravery to Orderly Sergeant.

Lucius T. Bushnell was born in the town of Butternuts, Dec. 15, 1839, and educated at the Gilbertsville Academy. He enlisted Dec. 19, 1863, as a private in Co. E., 2nd N. Y. H. A., at Norwich, N. Y., going from here to Elmira, to Washington, to Arlington Heights, thence to Fort Bennett; sent to hospital at Washington, and discharged from here Sept. 8, '64. Granted a furlough. went home, returned to, and joined his regiment near Petersburg, Va. Was promoted to Corporal and 2nd Lieut., receiving his commission while in the hospital and unable to muster. Feb. 20th, he was assigned to Co. A. After the surrender of Lee, was on duty at Fort Whipple, and on the third day of September, received his commission as 1st Lieutenant and assigned to Co. E., and in command of the company. He was a good soldier, and did faithful service in seventeen engagements. Was mustered out at Fort Whipple, Sept. 29, '65, receiving his final discharge at Rickers Island, Oct. 9, '65. He joined Musson Post, served as Senior Vice, and elected Commander for 1890 and '91. He is now residing at Gilbertsville with his family, a wife and son 25 years old.

Lewis M. Bryant was born at Gilbertsville, N. Y., April 9, 1832, and was educated at the Gilbertsville Academy. He enlisted in Aug. 1861, as a private in Houghtailing's Light Art., at Ottawa, Ill., and re-enlisted on the 2nd day of Oct., '61, at Gilbertsville, N. Y., as a private in Co. E., 2nd N. Y. H. A. Was taken prisoner near Deep Bottom, June 2nd, and sent to Libby Prison, and after eight days transferred to Andersonville, and from there sent to Milan Prison, near Macon, Ga. Was paroled and went to Annapolis and exchanged at Savannah, Ga. He was engaged in the battle of the Wilderness, the seven day's fight before Richmond, and was wounded in the knee at Cold Harbor, but refused to go to the hospital and remained in the field until the surrender of Lee at Appomattox. Was discharged in June, 1865, and returned to Gilbertsville, and to farming. Is a charter member of Musson Post. He is now residing near Gilbertsville, his family consisting of an estimable wife, four sons and a daughter.

Ferdinand Shaw was born on July 5, 1833, in the town of Butternuts, three miles east of Gilbertsville. His parents died during his tenth year; he was brought up by his uncle, Jared Comstock. He attended school and was fitted for college at the Gilbertsville Academy, entered Amherst College, and graduated with the class of '57, and accepted a position as assistant teacher in the Normal Academy, Chenango Co. He was afterwards tendered and accepted a more lucrative position as Principal of a boarding school at Ovid, Seneca Co., N. Y. While at Ovid the war of the rebellion broke out, and he was one of the first to respond to the President's call for troops, enlisting in April, 1861, as a private in the 12th Battery, N. Y. V. A short time after the arrival of the Battery at Washington he was promoted to the rank of Quartermaster-Sergt. He participated with the 12th Battery in several severe engagements, and at Reams' Station took charge, and brought off from the field their only remaining gun, the rest being captured by the enemy. On the 10th day of Aug., '64, he was commissioned Quartermaster, with the rank of Lieutenant; was mustered into the 98th N. Y. V., and was, with this regiment, the first troops to enter Richmond after its evacuation. He was for a time in charge of the old Libby Prison, which was used as a depot for Quartermaster and subsistence stores for the Union Army. For zeal, energy, and faithful discharge of duty he was promoted to Commissary of Subsistence, with the rank of Captain. His commission, signed by Abraham Lincoln, was dated Feb'y. 22nd, 1865. This, no doubt, was among the last he signed, as he was assassinated on the 14th of April following. He was attached to the staff of Brig. Gen. Ripley, commanding 1st Brig., 2nd Division 24th A. C. at Broad Rock, near Manchester, three miles from Richmond. Ordered to report to Gen. Devens, commanding Department of Northeastern Va., headquarters at Fredericksburg, where he remained as a member of his staff until mustered out of service in 1866. On the 15th of May, '66, he received a commission assigning him the rank of Major by brevet, signed by Andrew Johnson, then President. He was a model soldier, esteemed and respected by all who knew him. After his discharge he returned to

Gilbertsville, and was married in the following year, engaging in the mercantile business. He has been elected to many positions of honor and responsibility, educational, political and religious. Joined W. A. Musson Post as a charter member, and was Quartermaster until he died at his residence in Gilbertsville, March 10th, 1892. He was generous, confiding, and trusted in others, to the extent of his own purity of conscience. Was mourned by his companions in arms, and every citizen of the county admitted to the privacy of his friendship; by a brother and sister, a young wife and a son, George Ferdinand, aged 10 years, now residing at Gilbertsville, N. Y.

Charles A. Hurlburt was born at Gilbertsville, educated at the common school and the academy, and on leaving school, going on a farm. He enlisted in Aug. 1861, in Co. E., 2nd N. Y. H. A., and assisted in recruiting said company. Was mustered into the service at Staten Island, and ordered to report at Washington. The regiment remained in the fortifications, doing garrison duty until the Spring of 1864. Engaged in the second battle of Bull Run, was taken prisoner and paroled on the field. Promoted to 2nd Lieut. in February '64, and for meritorious conduct on the field was promoted in June, 1864, to 1st Lieut. He engaged in all the battles of the campaign, until they fought at Reems' Station. Here the 12th N. Y. lay at the left of his regiment; the guns were disabled, and he was ordered by Gen. Howard to take command; he nobly stood by the guns until too late to escape, and was again taken prisoner. He was sent to Richmond, remained two months, was paroled, and soon after exchanged. After his discharge from service, he sold musical instruments. In 1875, went on a farm, afterwards accepting a position as commercial traveler. His health failing, he returned to Gilbertsville and died in 1890. He was a true friend, of a genial disposition, and his memory is cherished by all who knew him.

J. Z. Shartz was born in the town of Guilford, Chenango Co., June 15, 1841. He attended the district school, going on a farm, and enlisted Sept. 22, '63, at Norwich, and was mustered into the service at Hearts Island as a recruit for Co. B., 90th Regt., N. Y. V. Joined the regiment at Cedar Creek on Friday, and the following Tuesday engaged in the battle of Cedar Creek, and was wounded in the right ankle; sent to hospital at Baltimore, and transferred to Summitt House, Philadelphia; discharged from the service June 7, '65. Is a charter member of Musson Post, has served as Quartermaster and Officer of the Day, and is at the present time Junior Vice Commander. He is now residing at Gilbertsville with his family, a wife and son aged 24.

Lloyd Shaw was born in the town of Butternuts, July 23, 1843, educated at the common schools and the academy; he enlisted Aug. 12, 1862, in Co. H., 121st Reg. N. Y. V.; was sent to the hospital at Hagerstown in the fall of 1862, remaining but a few weeks. He served faithfully with his regiment and did splendid service in thirty-two hard fought battles in which they had engaged. It is with much pride that he refers to the service of his regiment at Crampton Pass; Antietam, South Mountain, Gainsville, Brandy Station, the Wilderness, Second Bull Run, Cedar Run, front of Petersburg and Coal Harbor. At the battle of the Wilderness he carried Capt. Butts from the field; Was mustered out of the service Aug. 8, 1865; returned to Gilbertsville and went on a farm. Joined Musson Post in 1882; served as Quartermaster three years, and Senior Vice one year. He is now residing in Gilbertsville, with his family, a wife and two sons, ages 23 and 14.

William J. Smith was born in London, England, in 1829, coming to America in 1850. He attended evening school at Syracuse, N. Y., and learned the shoemaker trade, and located at Gilbertsville in the year 1860; he enlisted as a musician connected with the band of the 51st N. Y. V. Was discharged in 1862 and returned to Morris. In 1874 moved to Gilbertsville and joined Musson Post in 1882. Was elected collector for the town of Butternuts for 1891. He is now residing at Gilbertsville. Was engaged in the battles of Roanoke Island and Newbern, N. C.

John S. Kellogg was born at Gilbertsville in May, 1831. Educated at the academy; enlisted and went to the front as leader of the band for the 51st. Reg., N. Y. V.; was discharged by special order of the War Department, and received an appointment after the surrender of Lee, in the Commissary department, where he remained until the war closed. Joined Musson Post in 1890. Served as Sergeant-Major during 1891.

Hiram S. Cone was born at Wallingford, New Haven Co., Conn., in 1836; attended the common schools, and leaving school learned the shoemakers trade. He moved to Gilbertsville, N. Y., in 1858, and enlisted in the 51st N. Y. V. as a member of the band. Was discharged in 1862 by special order of the War Department. He joined the Post in 1891, and is now residing with his family at Gilbertsville, N. Y. He was engaged in the battle of Roanoke Island and Newbern, N. C.

OFFICERS OF MUSSON POST.

William Mungle, ...Commander.
E. L. Donaldson, ...Senior Vice-Commander.
J. Z Shartz, ...Junior Vice-Commander.
A. J. Cowan, ...Adjutant.
F. A. Shaw ....Quartermaster.
A. D. Dye, ...Chaplain.
T. H. Musson, ...Surgeon.
Scott Gilbert, ...Officer of the Day.
Lloyd Shaw, ...Officer of the Guard.
R. B Myrick, ...Sergeant-Major

Past Commanders

T. H. Musson,	J. D. Bloodgood,
R. B. Myrick,	A. J. Cowan,
A. D. Dye,	P. W. McIntier,
L. D. Bushnell.	

List of Members.

Babcock, Henry, ...(record unknown)
Borden, Eugene......................................A, 51, N. Y.
Bryant, L ....E, 2, N. Y. H. A.
Bellamy, J. C..................................B, 20, U. S. C. T
Bushnell, L. P.......................................E., 2, N. Y.
Cady, C. C...B, 114, N. Y.
Cowan, Andrew J ....K, 121, N. Y.
Cone, Hiram, musician..............................51 N. Y. V.
Dye, Alden D.....................................C, 114 N. Y.
Donaldson, E. L., musician ....51 N. Y. V.
Flint, Joseph F....................................K, 11 N. Y. .C
Foster, George ....C, 152 N. Y. V.
Gilbert, Scott...................................A, 114 N. Y. V.

Hammond, Henry T..................................E, 89 N. Y.
Jewell, James P.....................................F, 121 N. Y.
Kellogg, John S., musician......................51 N. Y. V.
Lamphere, Charles................................C, 114 N. Y.
Musson, T. H.......................................K, 161 N. Y.
Marvin, Pope.......................................K, 161 N. Y.
Mungle, William...................................E, 144 N. Y.
Myrick, R. B..2, Iowa Vol.
Shartz, J. Z...B, 90 N. Y.
Silvey, Samuel A..................................G, 152 N. Y.
Shaw, Lloyd..H, 121 N. Y.
Smith, Thomas K..................................K, 121 N. Y.
Smith, William J., musician,....................51 N. Y.
Stebbins, William E..............................G, 142
Webster, Edwin M................................K, 121

In Memoriam.

Gregory, Henry...................................G, 155 N. Y.
Genson, Johnson O..............................K, 121 N. Y.
Hurlbut, Chas A..................................E, 22 N. Y. A.
Murray, William...................................K, 121 N. Y.
Stewart, Anthony.................................E, 26 N. Y. C. T.
Shaw, F. A...42 N. Y. Bat
Truax, Silas J.....................................C, 16 N. Y. A.
Townsand, E. W..................................B, 144 N. Y.
Alsop, William.....................................E, 2 N. Y. H. A.
Cornell, Daniel....................................C, 114 N. Y.

Graves Decorated by W. A Musson Post, 223.

CIVIL WAR 1861--1865.

Alsop, William B.   Hastings, John T.

ALVA S. PEARSON,

DEALER IN

Groceries, Provisions, Crockery and Glassware,

Drugs, Paints and Oils,

Dye Stuffs, Tobacco, Cigars, Etc.,

SPECIALTIES.

* FINE TEAS AND COFFIES. *

Country Produce taken in exchange for Groceries.

Main St., Cherry Valley, N. Y.

R. BIERMAN,

DEALER IN

HARDWARE, TINWARE, STOVES,

HARNESS, TRUNKS, PAINTS, OILS, &C.

Harmony Row, (Oppo: Central House,)

CHERRY VALLEY, N. Y.

Harness Repairing neatly done.

Babcock, Frank
Brown, F. O.
Coss, Fred
Callahan, Chaplain
Clinton, Dewitt
Green, Augustus
Genson, F. O.
Gorton, Joshua
Gregory, Henry
Houghkirk, John
Hurlbutt, Chas. A.

Hastings, Geo. W.
Hastings, James K.
Jackson, James
Moulton, Samuel C.
Murray William
Musson, W. A.
Stuart, Anthony
Shaw, F. A.
Stebbins, Charles
Shew, L.
Truax, S. J.

Webb, Fletcher.

OTHER WARS.

Bryant, Alexander
Benedict, Isaac
Benedict, Mordecai
Brown, Elizur
Chittenden, Reuben
Cole, W. E.
Comstock, Jared
Coye, Asa
Cox, Thomas
Donaldson, Altemont

Goff, —— ——
Gilbert, Abijah
Lillie, Elisha
Lillie, Bradford
Leonard, Samuel
Nash, David
Palmer, Jared
Shaw, Col. David
Shaw, David
Shaw William

Townsend Jeremiah.

E. A. STERNBERG,

DEALER IN

BOOTS, SHOES, RUBBER GOODS,

UMBRELLAS, HATS, CAPS, &C.

The latest styles in Ladies' and Gents' Ties,

CHERRY VALLEY, N. Y.

Prices Reasonable.   **G. W. BRONSON,**   Gas Administered.

DENTIST

ARTIFICIAL TEETH A SPECIALTY

AND AT PRICES TO CONFORM WITH THE TIMES.

FILLING WITH GOLD, SILVER, PLATINA, Etc.,

AND GUARANTEED TO GIVE SATISFACTION.

Main Street,   - -   Cherry Valley, N. Y.

JOHN ✦ FEULNER,

Main Street,   - -   Cherry Valley, N. Y.

Fine Merchant Tailoring,

AND DEALER IN

First-Class Ready-Made Clothing.

All Work & Goods guaranteed as represented.

Emory Upton Post, No. 224,

South & Cherry Valley, N. Y.

Regular Meetings Second and Fourth Saturdays in each month at G. A. R. Hall.

THIS Post was organized, Charter received and mustered into the department of New York July 4, 1881, by Mustering Officer W. L. Knapp, of Johnson Post No. 25, Worcester, N. Y., assisted by Comrade C. E. Foot of Snyder Post, Cobleskill, N. Y., and other comrades from the Brown and Johnson Posts. David A. Finch was elected first Commander.

The Post was named in honor of the famous Tactician and distinguished soldier and scholar, Emory B. Upton, the gallant Colonel of the 121st Regiment, N. Y. V.

Are there soldiers, or civilians, conversant with the heroic deeds of the brave men who fought the battles of their country, who have not a vivid recollection of the brilliant victory achieved by the brave Upton and twelve picked regiments which he selected, (including his own, the 121st,) at the battle of Spottsylvania, May 10th, '64, to charge the enemy's works? Upton's clear voice rang out, "Attention, battalions! *Forward, double quick, charge!*" and a sheet of flame burst from the rebel lines, while the cannister from their artillery came crashing through the Union ranks, and scores, and hundreds of our brave fellows fell, literally covering the ground. But nothing daunted, the noble fellows (under his lead) rushed upon the defences, leaping over the ditch in front, and mount-

CAPTAIN HETHERINGTON DURING WAR TIMES; THE POSITION OF HAND AND SWORD WHEN STRUCK BY THE BULLET.

ing the breast-works. The rebels made a determined resistance, and a hand-to-hand fight ensued, until, with their bayonets, our men had filled the rifle pits with bleeding rebels. For distinguished services he was promoted to Brigadier-General and in Command of the 6th Corps, and Brevet Major-General U. S. A.

John E. Hetherington was born at Cherry Valley, N. Y., June 22, 1842, and was educated at the academy of that place. October 12, 1861, he enlisted in Company D, 1st Reg. U. S. Sharpshooters, Col. Berdan commanding. It was from no boyish freak, but from a deliberate sense of duty, that he left the then most extensive bee business in the land, and entered the service of his country. The spare time of the summer before had been spent in target-rifle practice, and his mother had made his under clothing previous to enlistment. But war is an easy thing to write about, but a terrible thing to deal with. Before one year had expired, of nine intimate friends from Cherry Valley who had entered the army, four were dead, four discharged for disability, and Capt. Hetherington alone remained in the service. Gen. Sheridan says, "Courage measures the power the mind has over the body." The Captain stood at his post in a most dangerous branch of the service, when most men would have been in the hospital, or discharged for disability. His army surgeon has left on record the following tribute to his bravery: "On the 12th day of May, 1864, at Spottsylvania, he became very much exhausted by reason of chronic diarrhea, but declined being relieved from duty; and although wounded in the head he heroically remained in command of his company." And again, "On the 18th day of June, 1864, in action before Petersburg, Va., he received a serious wound in the hand, which disabled him from duty. At the time of receiving said wound he was suffering from chronic diarrhea, and was so weak and debili-

L. W. THOMPSON & SON,

Practical Watchmakers and Jewelers,

AND DEALERS IN

Clocks, Watches, Jewelry and Silverware.

Optical Glasses a Specialty.

Repairing Neatly Executed.

Work Warranted as Represented.

MAIN STREET,

CHERRY VALLEY, N. Y.

WM. DRANE,

DEALER IN

Furniture, Upholstery, Undertaking,

Wooden and Willow Ware,

Groceries, Confections, Tobacco & Cigars.

Only Soda Fountain in Cherry Valley.

CANNED GOODS, — SALT AND DRIED MEATS.

Cherry Valley, N. Y.

tated by it that he was a better subject for the hospital than the battlefield." This was the wound received when his sword was shattered by a bullet, and a piece of the weapon was driven through his hand. The engraving shows this piece lying by the broken sword. The portrait

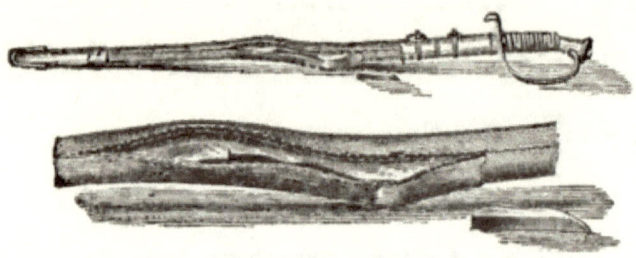

THE SWORD WHICH SAVED THE CAPTAIN'S LIFE.

shows the position of the sword and hand. He had for the moment thrown his rubber blanket* across the hilt of his sword, and then over his shoulder, very much as a tramp would carry his pack. Providentially the bullet, so well directed, found a lodgment in his sword and hand instead of his heart, which, you notice, lay just beneath. Major General Wilkinson, of the British Army, on seeing this sword, said that he had seen many of the heirlooms of prominent British families, and the relics sent home from twenty years of active service, and added, "Among them all there are none that I consider as fine a personal relic as this broken sword. The Captain threw this away as being of no further use to him; but it was preserved

---

*Before an engagement, an officer transfers to his darkey or servant all luggage—retaining only his rubber blanket and haversack, for use in case the aforesaid gentleman fails to put in an appearance after the fight. His blanket is made into a small role and tied at the ends, then carried across his shoulder and breast as a sash is worn. In hot weather this is oppressive; and for temporary relief, although in the midst of a hard fight, the Captain had tfirown his rubber across the hilt of his sword, and that across his shoulder.

R. G. WALROD,
General ✣ Merchandise ✣ Store,

Alden St., Cherry Valley, N. Y.

DRY GOODS,
Gents' Furnishings,
Ready-Made Clothing,

And everything pertaining to

:-: General :-: Merchandise. :-:

LIVERY STABLE,

GEO. W. MILLSON & SON, PROPRIETORS,

CHERRY VALLEY, N. Y.

(NEAR THE DEPOT.)

Double & Single Rigs at Reasonable Prices.

Telephone and Telegraph Orders Given Prompt Attention.

by his men. He also received a gunshot wound in the shoulder in the second battle of Bull Run, Aug. 29, 1862. Entering the service a private, he came out a Captain, in that division of the army when a captaincy meant in some ways as much as the command of a whole regiment would in some other branches of the service. A whole regiment of sharpshooters was seldom posted together; but companies were used instead of regiments. The sharpshooting service was a man-to-man conflict, and it required great care and skill in posting a company so that they would not be picked off by the opposing riflemen. The Captain of Co. D. was killed in the battle of Gettysburg, July 3, 1863, and Lieut. J. E. Hetherington was recommended for promotion by Col. Berdan, from the battle-field. At the close of the Gettysburg campaign, an order was sent to the commanding officers of the army to report to the Secretary of War the names of such officers and men as had distinguished themselves for bravery and meritorious conduct during the campaign. The name of J. E. Hetherington appears in the list, and furnishes the best of proof that his promotion was well earned. While in the army the Captain was in all the principal battles of the Army of the Potomac, besides many minor engagements which will never be recorded. He was discharged from the service, Sept. 20, 1864, by reason of disability from wounds received in action. For two years after, it was a question whether he would live; but he gradually regained a larger part of his former vigor. He has attended the State encampment for several years as a delegate from Emery Upton Post.

James D. Clyde, the present Commander, was born at Cherry Valley in Aug. 1843; attended the common schools, completing his education at Union College, and enlisted Sept. 15, 1861, as a private in Co. C, 44th Reg. N. Y. V.

Mustered in at Albany; was wounded at Hall's Hill and discharged June 17. 1862. He re-enlisted in Aug. 62, and was mustered into the service as First Lieut. of Co. G. 121st Reg. N. Y. V., and in command of company at South Mountain and Crampton Pass. Nov. 11, '63, was mustered in as 1st Lieutenant in Co. E, 76th Reg. N. Y. V., in command of company, and mustered out March 11, '64, to be mustered in as Captain of Co. D, 76th Reg. He was a distinguished soldier, and served with great zeal and devotion to duty. No officer in the regiment stood higher in the estimation of both officers and men, than did Capt. Clyde. He was taken prisoner in the Wilderness and sent to Lynchburg, to Macon and Savannah, Ga., thence to Charleston, S. C., and placed here under the fire of the Union guns, and finally taken to Charlotte and exchanged at Wilmington. Was mustered out by special order of the War Department, March 12, 1865, he being a supernumerary officer, by reason of the consolidation of the 44th and 76th Regiments. Returned to Cherry Valley, graduated at the college of Physicians and Surgeons at 4th Ave. and 23rd Streets, New York, and engaged in the drug business in Cherry Valley. In the spring of 1891, disposing of his business interests, he is at the present time engaged in raising fancy stock. He joined Col. Upton Post and was elected Commander for 1882 and '83 '90-'91 and '92. That the Post retains its standing is largely due to his efforts. His time and means are at the Post's command, and on each recurring Memorial Day, through his personal supervision, a profusion of flowers, and the flag for which they fought, are placed upon more than fifty graves. He is Past-Master of Cherry Valley Lodge 334, and member of Otsego Chapter, Cooperstown, and an honored and respected citizen of Cherry Valley, N. Y.

Norman W. Herdman was born at Canajoharie, N. Y., attended the common school, and completed his education at a select school at that place. In 1850, went to Cherry Valley, and engaged in the grocery businesf. While here he enlisted as a private in Co. G, 121st N. Y. V.; sent to Washington, joined McClellan on his march to Antietam, participating in battle at Crampton Gap, held the Gap for two days, and went to Bakerville; was here taken with typhoid fever and sent to Cemetery Hospital at Hagerstown. Joined his regiment Dec. 15., at Aquia Creek; engaged in the battle of Fredericksburg, re-crossed the river and went into camp at White Oak church for winter quarters. In January was with Burnside during his Mud March; May 3, was at the battle of Salem church, was taken prisoner, sent to Richmond, and was prostrated by sun-stroke on the way; was placed in the Pemberton Tobacco factory, and on Bell Island; sent from there to Annapolis, and to Convalescent Camp as a paroled prisoner; then sent to regiment without exchange; to camp near Brandy Station; in the spring of 1864, to the Wilderness; May 5th engaged in battle; the 5th and 6th, was with the 6th Corps; was injured here and sent to Harwood Hospital, Washington, and transferred to Chester General Hospital, thence to Turner Hospital, Philadelphia, and from here sent to his regiment at Cedar Creek the middle of Oct. 1864; thence to front of Petersburg, participating in battle; engaged in first battle of Hatches Run; remained on the lines at Petersburg until the picket lines were advanced, and fought the battle of Fort Fisher March 25, participating in the final charge on the night of the 1st of April. The 2nd Brigade went to the right in front of the 9th Corps, and through Fort Hall, going into Petersburg before daylight; went in pursuit of Gen. Lee, and April 6th fought the battle of Sailor Creek; next morning continued in pursuit of Lee, until he surrendered at Appomattox; went with the 6th Corps to Dansville. At the close of the campaign was promoted to Sergeant-Major; mustered out June 25, 1865 at Halls Hill. Returned to Cherry Valley, appointed Deputy County Clerk of Otsego county, and appointed to a position in the Insurance department at Albany. Joined Upton Post, March 24, 1883, and elected Commander for 1887. He is now residing at Cherry Valley with his family, an estimable wife and daughter, now attending school at Cherry Valley, N. Y.

John M. Lovejoy was born at Roseboom, May 25, 1843. He attended school until 16 years old, then went on a farm. Aug. 7, 1862, he left the farm to enlist as a private in Co. G, 121st N. Y. V. He did splendid service with his regiment at Winchester, Fisher Hill and Cedar Creek; was wounded at Charleston, Aug. 21, 1864; sent to Baltimore, Md., and soon after transferred to Chestnut Hill, Philadelphia; while here he received a furlough for twenty days; returned to his regiment Dec: 25, 1864, was promoted and acted as Color Guard to the regiment until discharged June 25, 1865. Returned to Roseboom; went on a farm, but he never fully recovered from the effects of his wound, and in 1870 left the farm and went into the general agency business. Joined Upton Post at South Valley as charter member; served as Adjutant for seven years and Quartermaster two years. He has been Justice of the Peace for ten years at South Valley, N. Y.

William Huddleston was born Jan. 21, 1832, in Albany Co., N. Y., educated at Albany, and enlisted Nov. 2nd, 1861, as a private in Co. D, Berdan's 1st Reg. U. S. S. S. A grateful nation will, as long as time shall last, remember with gratitude the faithful service rendered by this regiment during the conflict from 1861 to 1865. Huddleston's record is that of the regiment, serving with great devotion to duty until discharged Nov. 22nd, 1864, in front of Petersburg. Returned to Roseboom and married the second daughter of William Raway, Sep. 19th, 1865. He died at Cherry Valley Jany. 26, 1886, and was buried under the auspicies of the G. A. R. Post and the Order of Odd Fellows. He left a wife and son George, who died Aug. 16, 1891.

Edwin M. Hunt was born in Westerloo in 1843, and enlisted in Aug., 1864 as a recruit for Co. G, 121st N. Y. V., joining his regiment at Bakersville, Va., and was wounded at Cedar Creek Oct. 9th, '64. He joined Upton Post in 1883.

John C. Milson was born at Cherry Valley April 23rd, 1836; enlisted in Aug. 62, as a private in Co. G, 121st N. Y. V. He was a brave soldier, and did splendid service, engaging in all the battles and skirmishes of his regiment until they were discharged June 25th, '65.

John Story was born in Columbia Co., in July, 1821. going with his parents when four years old to Cherry Valley, and enlisting at Albany, N. Y., Aug. 28, '64, as a recruit for Co. G, 151st N. Y. V., joining the regiment at Cedar Creek Oct. 17th, and two days after participating in the battle of Cedar Creek, and Oct. 24 in the first battle of Hatches Run. He was a brave soldier and color bearer from Oct. '64 until his regiment was discharged. He returned to Cherry Valley, where he has since resided.

Philip Wales was born in England, sailing for America and locating at Cherry Valley, N. Y., in 1830, and enlisting Aug. 4th, in Co. D, 6th N. Y. C. at Staten Island. Was ordered to Fortress Monroe, arriving at Yorktown April 29, '62, remaining here until the evacuation, May 4, '62; then going down the peninsula, engaging in the battle of Williamsburg; after this to Falls Creek, taking

Clark Hardendorf & Son,
Alden St. Meat Market.

Meats and Vegitables,
Prime Sausage, Fresh Lard,
Choice Salt and Dried Meats,
Poultry, Oysters and Clams in their Season,

Union Block, Cherry Valley, N. Y.

C. M. LAWYER,
MANUFACTURER OF AND DEALER IN
HARNESS OF ALL KINDS,
Alden St., next to Fonda's Shoe Store,
CHERRY VALLEY, N. Y.

Whips, Brushes, Fly Nets, Lap Robes, Horse Sheets, Harness Oil, Axle Grease, Soaps, Ear Tabs, Horse Furnishing Goods of every nature and style.

REPAIRING NEATLY EXECUTED.

P. V. GENTER & SON,
COOPERS.

Manufacturing and Repairing of
Barrels, - Tubs, - Cisterns, - Etc.
—)ALL KINDS OF(—
TURNING AND SCROLL SAWING.
Wall Street, Cherry Valley, N. Y.

part in the battle of June 1, '62, and in the 7 days' battles from Mechanicsville to Malvern Hill, July 1st, '62. Company's D, A, K, and F, were detached from the regiment at Perryville and ordered to report to Gen. Sumner, in front of Yorktown; arrived at Harrison Landing in July; thence to Alexandria, taking part in Pope's campaign. Was with McClellan at Antietam; thence to Harpers Ferry. Was for distinguished services promoted to Captain and transferred to Co. F; was with Gen. Keys at Yorktown, and scouting up and down the peninsula. The squadron was ordered in Sept. '63 to join the regiment at Racoon Ford on the Rapidan, and crossing the river, upon a piece of rising ground to the left, a battery had taken a position. Here the bravery of the 6th N. Y. Cavalry was demonstrated, under the lead of their old commander, Gen. Devens. Major Hall gave the order to "Draw saber! *Charge!*" There was no wavering; right into the storm of shot and shell they rode, and through their broken ranks, striking heavy blows to the right and left. Wheeling to the right they reformed and charged the second time; Capt. Wales was dismounted and injured, the 6th losing 30 men in killed and wounded. Capt. Wales was a brave soldier, always caring for the comforts of his men. His record is that of his regiment, serving faithfully until discharged June 25, 1865. He returned to Cherry Valley, where he is now residing, an honored and respected citizen, serving as a Justice of the Peace.

The town of Cherry Valley, where the names of the lamented Col. Alden, Elizabeth Dickson and Elanor McKinney, who were massacred Nov. 11, 1778, stand preeminent, is of historic fame, made so, not only from the fact that within its boundaries has been demonstrated the patriotism and valor of those of the Anglo Saxon race, but in later years, by the heroic deeds and distinguished services of her brave sons during the civil war from 1861 to '65. Cherry Valley has added another and a bright page to her history, and to the fidelity and courage of those who participated in the conflict for the perpetuation of a free and independent nation It is no disparagement to the veterans now residing at Cherry Valley, or those who have passed away, to say, that in the person of Egbert Olcott we find one of the coolest and bravest soldiers enlisting from Otsego County, born at Cherrey Valley Dec. 21, 1836. When the first call for troops was made he raised a company, which was not accepted. He then enlisted as a private in Co. C, 44th N. Y. V.; was commissioned 2nd Lieutenant; Nov. 26, '61, promoted to 1st Lieut., and assigned to the 25th Reg.; promoted to Capt. Aug. 23, '62; transferred to and assisted in organizing the 121st Reg., and promoted to Major. He knew no fear, was always in the thickest of the fight, leading and cheering his men to battle. For bravery he was again promoted in April, 1863, to Col., and discharged with his regiment at Halls Hill June 25, 1865. He died Feb. 23, 1861, and was buried at Cherry Valley, N. Y., and his grave is the shrine of his comrades on each recurring 30th of May.

Among the brave soldiers now residing there, we would mention Henry C. Weeks, born in Westchester Co. in 1843. After receiving a common school education he went on a farm, and enlisted in 1862, as a private in Co. E, 135th N. Y. V., (after re-organizing as the 6th N. Y. H. A.) Was ordered to Baltimore and thence to Harpers Ferry, where he remained during the winter. Feb. 1836, joined the army of the Potomac at Brandy Station; received a bayonet wound in the knee at Bull Run, when returning to Manasses Junction from a reconnoisance, and sent to Lincoln hospital at Washington, and transferred to David's Island, New York; he remained three months, when he rejoined his regiment at Brandy Station. ready and eager for the campaign of 1864. Was through the Wilderness, the Seven day's fight, and in front of Petersburg with the 6th Corps to reinforce Gen. Sheridan in the Shanandoah Valley; participating in the battle of Winchester Sept. 19th, and for bravery was promoted to Sergt.; and at Cedar Creek, Oct. 19, '64, when he lost a leg, was sent to Baltimore, and from here to the Camden St. Hospital at Philadelphia; discharged June 9, 1865. Returned to Winchester, where he was for three years engaged in the butcher business. Went to Brooklyn, was employed in the postoffice for three years, and received an appointment under the city government. In 1876, returned to Winchester, going to Sharon Springs in 1883. Was employed in the legislative department at Albany during the winters of 1886 to '89; locating in Cherry Valley in the fall of 1890, he accepted a position as clerk for one of the dry goods houses, and in the fall of '91 ac- accepting a similar position in the employ of William Drane. He was a model soldier, of a genial disposition, a true friend and respected citizen, who has made many and untold sacrifices that his country might live. He is now residing with his family, wife, two sons and three daughters, at Cherry Valley, N. Y.

II. Irving Baker was born at Cherry Valley, N. Y., in Sept. 1842. After leaving school he accepted a clerkship in Cherry Valley, soon after accepting a similar position at Palatine Bridge, N. Y. He enlisted in Sept. 1851 as a private in Co. H, 76th Reg., N. Y. V., going to the front at once, and participating in the battles of Gainsville, second Bull Run, South Mountain, Antietam, Snickers Gap, Fredericksburg, Va., Chancellorsville, and was wounded at the battle of Gettysburg, July, 1863, and sent to Saterlee Hospital, Philadelphia. April 1864, started for the Wilderness, engaging at the battle of Coal Harbor; was here wounded, but remained with the regiment, and was again wounded in front of Petersburg June 18, '64. He was carried from the field by Albert Gross, and an ambulance procured, he was sent to hospital. He displayed undaunted courage at Gettysburg. The powder in the cannon tubes had become so damp from exposure to the rains of the preceding night that the pieces could not be discharged. In the midst of a most terrific fire, Sergeant Baker, with cool and steady nerve, picked out the damp powder from the primed guns. This was done in the hottest of the fighting, and while our dead and wounded were falling around and against him. After his discharge he removed to Cherry Valley in 1866, was employed in the North Woods as a civil engineer, accepting a position in 1867 on the eastern division of the Midland R. R., (now the Ontario & Western,) and in 1872 on the Rochester and State Line R. R. He was married in 1872 and located at Sandusky, Cattaragus Co. Went to Nebraska and in the spring of 1887 to Vincennes, Ind., as a civil engineer. He died Dec. 1, 1891, at Cherry Valley, N. Y., and was buried with military honors in the Cherry Valley Cemetery, leaving a wife, son and two daughters, now residing at Sandusky, N. Y.

Richard Bierman was born in Germany, coming to America in 1853, and located at St. Johnsville, N. Y., where he worked at harness making. In 1858 he moved to Oneida, then to Morrisville, Jefferson Co., two years after going to Camden, from which place he enlisted as a private in Co. F, 153rd N. Y. V., to battle for the country to which he had sworn allegiance but a few years before. He was mustered in at Fonda, N. Y., in Oct. 1862, and ordered to Alexandria, Va.; to Washington, to New Orleans, up the Red River expedition and through the Shanandoah Valley campaign to Savannah, Ga., participating in the battles at Sabine Cross Roads, Pleasant Hill, Cane River, crossing to Marksville Plains, Winchester and at Cedar Creek. Receiving his discharge Oct. 2nd, '65, he returned to St. Johnsville, going into the harness business; was burned out in 1873, moving to Cherry Valley and going into the same business; in 1880 enlarging his business by putting in a line of hardware goods; he was again burned out March 29, 1891, and is now erecting one of the finest blocks in Cherry Valley to accommodate his increasing trade, which he will occupy in July, 1892. He is a thorough business man, an honored and respected citizen and neighbor. He is residing with his family, consisting of wife and son Charles, aged 19, now in the employ of his father.

James J. Fonda was born at Schenectady in 1829. Going to the sunny South in 1853, and returning to Cherry Valley in 1855, he enlisted in Aug. 1861 in Co. C, — Reg. N. Y. V.; was mustered in at Staten Island. His record is that of his regiment, engaging in all the battles and skirmishes and always at his post, with the exception of about two weeks; he was taken with fever at Malvern Hill near the close of the Seven day's fight, and sent to City Hall Barracks, New York; again joining his regiment before leaving Harrison's Landing, was detailed as Ordinance Sergeant in charge of ammunition for the Division, until he was discharged. Returned to Cherry Valley and went into the shoe business in 1875. He is now residing with his family, a wife and three daughters and two sons.

R. G. Walrod was born in Cherry Valley in 1829, and was educated at the common schools. In 1855 he went South, locating at Falls Church, Va. The Southern people had enrolled his name, with others, for the service. After the shooting of Col. Elsworth, he came North, to Otsego Co., and was soon after appointed Purveyor of the 2nd Division, 12th Army Corps, in which position he remained until the close of the war. Taking up his residence in Cherry Valley, he engaged in the general merchandise business, in which he has, by strict attention to business and fair dealing, built up a handsome trade. He is of a social and agreeable disposition, a true friend and respected citizen.

POST OFFICERS.

James D. Clyde, ...Commander.
Alonzo Cady, ...Senior Vice-Commander.
James Hetherington, ...Junior Vice-Commander.
Norman W. Herdman, ...Adjutant.
John M. Lovejoy, ...Quartermaster.
Jacob Saulsbury, ...Surgeon.
E. B. Thompson, ...Chaplain.
Harrison Hadsell, ...Officer of the Day.
James Armstrong, ...Officer of the Guard.

PAST COMMANDERS.

| D. A. Finch, | James D. Clyde, | Amenzo Cady, |
| N. W. Herdman, | O. A. Brown, | Allen Lovejoy. |

LIST OF MEMBERS.

Armstrong, James.....................................I, 156 N. Y.
Baum, Henry...
Butler, John L ....I, 62 N. Y.
Bullis, Archibald......................................G, 121 N. Y.

Buck, Ezekial..
Brown, Oscar A............I, 152 N. Y.
Bush, Joseph............76 N.Y.
Butler, Edward W, 2nd Lieut............I, 132, N. Y.
Cady, Amenzo............C, 134 N. Y.
Clyde, James D., G, 121 N. Y............E, 76 N. Y.
Campbell, William............I, C, N. Y. C.
Ely, Darwin S............
Gross, Albert............H, 76 N. Y.
Galt, John S............
Hadsell, Harrison............
Hartom, Daniel............G, 121 N. Y.
Hetherington, James D............1st Reg. S. S.
Herdman, Norman W............G, 121 N. Y.
Hunt, Edwin M............G, 121 N. Y.
Howe, Jesse W............
Hubbard, John F............H. Art.
Hetherington, John E., Capt......D, Berdan's 1st U. S. S. S.
Hamlin, John J............I, 152 N. Y.
Head, Delos............D, C. N. Y. Cav.
Kniskern, Lyman P............K, 1st N. Y. Art.
Lovejoy, John M............G, 121 N. Y.
Lewis, Charles H............E, 22 N. Y.
Lovejoy, Allen............G, 121 N. Y. C. 22 Bat. V. R. C.
Mabie, David A............I, 152 N. Y.
Milson, John C............G, 121 N. Y. V.
Michaels, P. H............3rd N. Y. Art.
Neal, William J............
Ostrander, George............
Roe, Martin L............76 N. Y.
Risedorph, John H............D, 46 N. Y.
Story, John,............G, 121 N. Y.
Skimon, John............G, 121 N. Y.
Salisbury, Jacob............G, 121 N. Y.
Stafford, John............B, 5 N. Y. C.

Thompson, Erastus B..........................G, 121 N. Y.
Waldruff, Asa M................................K, 152 N. Y.
Walker, John E.................................E, 46 N. Y
Wales, Phillip R., Capt.......................F, 6 N. Y. C.

In Memoriam.

Butler, Hiram.........Died Aug. 31, 1885,.........I, 152 N. Y.
Campbell, James...... " Feb. 24, 1886,.........G, 121 N. Y.
Ferguson, Alex D... " Nov. 10, 1889,...A, 1st N. Y. L. A.
Huddleston William. " June 26, '86,.........1st U. S. S. S.
Oaks, Eli............... " Feb 26, 1886,.........G, 121 N. Y.
Smith, Moses G ...... " Feb. 25, 1861,......... E, 4 Wis.

GRAVES DECORATED BY COL. UPTON POST.

WAR OF 1861—1865.

Baker, Irving	Hodge, Chas E
Barnard Phineus	Harris, William
Botsford, John F	Howe, Joseph B
Barker, John	Hardendorf, Jacob
Bradford ———	Kirk, James
McLean, Chas. Capt	McLean, Chas. Wm
Morse, Francis Capt	McCoddack ———
Beaumont, John	Moore, James
Ballard, John W	Nelson, George
Bates, Samuel	Nichols, Chas. P
Chaddenden, Childs D	Olcott, Col. Egbert
Campbell, C. J. Genl	Craft, Wm. Capt

Drake, Samuel
Dauiels, John
Oakes, Eli Lieut
Engle, Geo P
Ferguson, H T
Scott, George
Sherman, James
George, James
Herdman, Geo A
Hardendorf, Cornelius
VanSlyke, Edwd Capt
Wilson, Jabez D

Drake, Nelson
Olcott, Delos W. Capt
Oakes, Perry
Reed, Dwight
Story, Robert
Fox, J S
Swan, Amos Brev Lt Col
Hubbard, Jessie
Hubbard, Augustus
Van DeBogart, Geo
Wallace, John
Wales, Edward

OTHER WARS.

Alden, Col E. massacred Nov. 11, '78.
Brien, Thomas.
Campbell, Sam'l Col
Elizabeth, Dickson
Fern, John
Hawver, Thomas
Ladman, Samuel
Nelson, William
Stearns, William
Warner ———

Campbell, Jessie
Clyde, Samuel
Eleanor, McKinney
Hamilton, ———
Gilday, Daniel
Levering, Thomas
Paddock, William
Sherman, James
Wilson Thomas

Elizabeth Dickson, massacred Nov. 11, 1778.
Eleanor McKinney, massacred Nov. 11, 1778.

LARD.  POULTRY.

The Finest and Most Tender Cuts

Of all kinds of Fresh Meat

—)CAN BE FOUND AT(—

THE MORRIS MARKET

I. C. CAREY, CARVER,

C. H. LAWRENCE, PROPRIETOR,

Brick Block, Main Street,

MORRIS, - New York.

—THE—

NEW CENTRAL HOTEL,

COOPERSTOWN, ◊ N. ◊ Y.

THIS House is new and the successor of the old Central so well and favorably known to the public. Under the present management all of the desirable features of the old stand will be retained, and many new ones added. Good rooms, well furnished. The table is not excelled by any other house. All the modern improvements, including electric light throughout the house.

LARGE STABLES CONNECTED WITH THE HOUSE.

W. M. POTTER, - - Proprietor.

George Kidder Post, No. 224,
MORRIS, N. Y.

Regular Meetings First and Third Saturday of each month, at G. A. R Hall.

GEORGE KIDDER Post was organized, its charter received, and mustered in to the department of New York on the 29th day of March, 1872, by R. L. Fox, commander of E. D. Farmer Post, Oneonta, as mustering officer, assisted by the officers of that post.

 Parley McIntier was born in the town of New Lisbon, Otsego County, December 26, 1829, and received his education at Pittsfield, N. Y. Leaving school he went to work on a farm. When an imperiled country called for help, he, like many other—patriotic sons, dropped the plow in the furrow, and enlisted August 4, 1862, as a private in Co. I, 121 N. Y. V., was mustered in to the U. S. service at camp Schuyler, Herkimer, N. Y., August 23, 1862. He was sent to hospital in October, '62, where he remained until May 3, '63, rejoining his regiment, and was with them in the thickest of the fight, and on the march, participating in every action until the 19th day of October, 1864, when he was wounded at Cedar Creek, Va., by a bullet shot through both thighs, and sent to Jarvis hospital, Baltimore, remaining until February 18, 1865, when he was discharged. Returned to Morris and to farming; was charter member—in fact, organizer—of the George Kidder Post No. 26, and was elected first commander. In 1884 he took a card from this post and joined W. A. Musson Post at Gilbertsville, and was elected commander in 1885: in April, 1890, rejoined the Kidder Post by transfer card from Musson Post, and again elected commander for the present year, 1892. His administration of the Post affairs are conducted to the satisfaction of his comrades, and credit to himself. He is now residing with his family, consisting of wife, two daughters, ages 15 and 13, and two sons, ages 7 and 9, at Morris N. Y.

William E. Southern was born at Morris, May 19, 1847, was educated at the common schools, leaving school when only 15 years old, to enlist as a private in Co C, 152d Regiment N. Y. V., August 30, 1862. Was mustered into the service at Camp Schuyler, and ordered to the defence of Washington, and from here to Suffolk, and thence to Yorktown, to White House Landing; back to Yorktown, through Williamsburg to Washington. Ordered to New York during the riot in July '63; in October ordered to the Army of the Potomac; was wounded in the ankle last day of the Wilderness Fight, sent to Army Square hospital, Washington, remaining nine months. He was a brave soldier, always on duty, and serving with distinction throughout. Was discharged Feb. 27, 1864; returned to Morris and joined Kidder Post as a charter member. He was first elected Commander to serve during the year 1880. His administration was most successful and he was elected each year until 1887. He was again placed in the chair in 1889, and served until 1892. He left the affairs of the Post at the end of his eleventh year as Commander, ranking second to none in the department.

Olney Brailey was born in the town of Butternuts, near Morris, in April 1856; attended the District school, completing his education at the Gilbertsville Academy.

He taught school winters for 15 years, during the summer working on a farm. He left the farm to enlist as a private in Co. E, 2nd N. Y. H. A., was mustered into the service and sent to the defence of Washington. Was discharged May 15, '64, for general disability. Returned to Butternuts, accepted a position as engineer on the steamer Teller, running between New York and Galveston, Texas; again locating at Morris, N. Y., and engaged in farming. He joined Musson Post at Gilbertsville in 1886, taking a transfer card and joined Kidder Post. He was elected Commander for 1888, and has served as Adjutant since that time.

William J. Cummings was born at New Lisbon, May 22, 1834, his parents going to Fly Creek when he was seven years old, in 1852 returning to New Lisbon, where he was educated at the common schools; afterwards going on a farm. He, like many of our country's defenders, left the farm to enlist, on the 29th of Sept., 1872, as a recruit for Co. D, 8th N. Y. Cavalry; was mustered in at Albany; ordered to New York, thence to Philadelphia, to Hagerstown, to Harpers Ferry, then to Richmond, arriving just before the seven day's fight, engaging in the battle at Gettysburg, Hagerstown, Fallen Water, Brandy Station, back to the Rappahannock, then detailed to the Cavalry Corps Hospital as Quartermaster. Remained here until the surrender of Lee; sent to Washington, and mustered out of service; met the Colonel, and was persuaded by him to go to Clouds Mills and then to Rochester to be mustered out with the regiment. Returned to New Lisbon and joined Kidder Post in 1882. Has served as Sen. and Jun. Vice Com., Chaplain and Officer of the Guard. He is now residing at New Lisbon with his family, consisting of a wife, two sons aged 23 and 18, and a daughter aged 20.

James Southern was born at Laurens in Dec. 1838, going to Morris with his parents when five years old; was educated at the district schools, and found employment on the farm. Aug. 29, 1862, he enlisted as a private in Co. C, 152nd N. Y. V., and was mustered in at Camp Schuyler; ordered to Washington, to Fort Ethen Allen, remaining until spring of 1863; was then sent to Yorktown, to Suffolk on the Black Water, then up the James River, to within eighteen miles from Richmond; and while on the march in June '63 towards Fredericksburg, the draft riots began in New York and the regiment was ordered to proceed to that city at once. Returned to Washington in 1862, and joined the Army of the Potomac, going to Miles Run, and back to Brandy Station; was here taken with typhoid fever and sent to regimental hospital; May 3, '64, sent to Armory Square hospital, Washington, and discharged Dec. 12, 1865. His record is that of his regiment, until he was sent to the hospital. He was a charter member of Kidder Post, and has served as Sen. and Jun. Vice Commander, Adjutant and Quartermaster of the Post. He is now residing at Morris, N. Y., with his son George R.; a daughter, Mrs. Frances Hathaway, is now residing at Laurens, and two sons are living at New Berlin.

Judson K. Davis was born at Middlefield, Otsego Co., N. Y., June 12, 1845; moved to Morris when nine years old, and attended the common schools. He enlisted in September, 1862, as a private in Co. G, 152nd N. Y. V., and was mustered at Camp Schuyler; going to the front and remaining with his regiment until they were discharged, his record being that of his regiment. He was discharged in July, 1865, and returned to Morris and went on a farm: joined Kidder Post in 1883, and has served as Officer of the Guard. He is now residing at Morris, N. Y., with his wife, and daughter aged 22, and son aged 15, one son aged 24 residing at Syracuse, N. Y., and a daughter, Mrs. Ira Sergeant, residing at Morris, N. Y.

Albert Becker has the honor and distinction of being the first man enlisting from the town of Morris, going to the front with the 1st N. Y. V. He was a first-class machinist, and left a good position and good wages to serve his country, and did splendid service for the right. Was twice wounded; once in the mouth, taking out part of the jaw and seven teeth, and once in the thigh. Was captured, and endured untold hardships within the walls of Libby Prison. He enlisted as a private, but for bravery was promoted to corporal, serving until the war ended. He is now residing in Newton, Harvey county, Kansas.

Peter Becker was also a brave soldier, enlisting as a member of the 14th N. Y. H. A. as private and promoted to corporal. He was in all the battles, skirmishes and marches of his regiment. His coat and vest were torn from his body by one of the shells of the enemy, but he escaped, going through the war without receiving a wound, although participating in many hard-fought battles. At the close of the war he was appointed a police detective; going west, he engaged in battle with the Indians, and by killing a chief gained a victory for the U. S. troops. For this service he was tendered by the government a position in the regular army, which he declined. He is now residing in Kingman, Kansas, having many friends at Morris, N. Y.

Elijah Thurston, Quartermaster of the post, was born at Gilbertsville, N. Y., in November, 1839, receiving his education at the common schools, and enlisting from the town of Morris, Oct. 16, 1862, in Co. C, 152d N. Y. V., and mustered in at Camp Schuyler. He was a faithful

W. W. Dilworth,
THE TAILOR,
MORRIS, - Otsego Co., - N. Y.

—THE LATEST STYLES IN—

Kersey's Cheviots, Meltons *
 * *   And Diagonals for

Suits, Overcoats and Trousers

Made to Order in the Latest Style.

☞ Perfect Fit Guaranteed. ☜

MRS. E. L. PAYNE,
DEALER IN

Dry Goods and Millinery,

BOOTS, SHOES, HATS, CAPS,
WALL PAPER & STATIONERY.

Paid up subscription for one year to the

GOOD FORM

PUBLISHERS PRICE $2.00,

PRESENTED TO CUSTOMERS
When their purchases amount to $10,

MORRIS, - N. Y.

and attentive soldier, engaging in all the marches, skirmishes and battles with his regiment, and for meritorious conduct was promoted at Munson Hil from private to mounted orderly sergeant in the brigade staff; was thrown from his horse at Munson Hill, disabled and sent to the hospital, remaining three months. Discharged July 25, 1865. Returned to Morris, N. Y. Joined Kidder Post in 1879; has served as Junior Vice Commander and Quartermaster for several years. He is now residing at Morris with his family—wife and son, aged 22.

Edwin P. Carr was born at Laurens, Feb. 10, 1853; was educated at the common schools. and afterward went on a farm. He enlisted at Morris as a recruit for Co. II, 169th N. Y. V. Joined the regiment at Chapin's Farm in August, 1864, where he remained three months; went to Fort Fisher and was blown up by the explosion of a powder magazine and sent to McDougal Hospital, New York, and soon after transferred to Troy Hospital, and discharged in June, 1865. He joined Kidder Post in 1874.

Sedate Foote, born at Morris. N. Y., June 29, 1836. After receiving a common school education he went on a farm, and left the farm to enlist as a private in Co. I, 121st Reg. N. Y. V., Aug. 4, 1862. He was engaged in all the battles and skirmishes of this regiment, the famous 121st, (one of the bravest in the Army,) and in the memorable battle of Cold Harbor, June 2, 1864, he was wounded and sent to Lincoln Hospital, Washington, thence to Davids Island, to City Point, and from here to Alexandria; remained in the hospital three weeks, and did guard druty at Alexandria until he was discharged July 13, 1865. Returned to Morris and joined Kidder Post in 1882. Has served as Officer of the Day and Sergeant of the Guard. He is now residing with his family at Morris, N. Y.

David C. Winton was born at Morris in 1837, and enlisted in the Band attached to the 51st Reg. N. Y. V. When they were discharged he re-enlisted as a member of the Band of the 2nd Brig., 6th Corps; was discharged July 1865; joined Kidder Post as a charter member; was elected Commander to succeed P. McIntier's first term, and served for two years. He is now residing at Morris with his family, consisting of wife, son and two daughters. One son is residing at Binghamton, and a daughter, Mrs. F. E. Warner, is residing at Unadilla, N. Y.

Parley McIntier was born in the town of New Lisbon, Otsego Co., Dec. 26, 1839, and received his education at Pittsfield, N. Y. Leaving school, he went to work on a farm; when an imperilled country called for help, he, like many other patriotic sons, dropped the plough in the furrow, and enlisted Aug. 4, 1862, as a private in Co. I, 121st N. Y. V.; was mustered into the U. S. service at Camp Schuyler, Herkimer, N. Y,, Aug. 23, 1862. He was sent to hospital in Oct. '62, where he remained until May 3, '63, rejoining his regiment, and was with them in the thickest of the fight and on the march, participating in every action until the 19th of Oct. 1864, when he was wounded at Cedar Creek, Va., by a bullet-shot through both thighs, and sent to Jarvis Hospital, Baltimore, remaining until Feb. 18th, 1865, when he was discharged. Returned to Morris and to farming; was charter member (in fact the organizer) of the George Kidder Post No. 61, and was elected first Commander. In 1883, he took a card from this Post and joined W. A. Musson Post at Gilbertsville, and was elected Commander in 1889; in April, 1890, re-joined the Kidder Post by transfer card from Musson Post, and was again elected Commander for the present year, 1892. His administration of the Post's affairs are conducted to the satisfaction of his comrades and credit to himself. He is now residing with his family, consisting of wife and two daughters ages 15 and 13, and two sons, ages 7 and 9, at Morris, N. Y.

A MEMBER OF UPTON POST.

Albert Gross was born at Cherry Valley, N. Y., received a common school education, and learned the carpenter trade. He enlisted in Sept. 1861, as a private in Co. H, 76th N. Y. V., was mustered into the service at Cherry Valley, going to Albany, thence to Washington. He was a true soldier, always careful to know what his duty was, and then to do it. Was with his regiment on the march and in the bloody battles from Rappahannock Station until the surrender of Lee at Appomattox. Whether at Gettysburg, where the regiment met its greatest loss; in the Wilderness when they had two color-bearers killed and three wounded; at Spotsylvania where the Brigade Commander was mortally wounded, or in any of the twenty-six battles in which they fought, by their gallantry and patriotism, proved themselves worthy of the historic figures emblazoned on their colors. He was color-bearer at Five Forks, and until the surrender of Lee, serving faithfully with his regiment, re-enlisting in the 147th, and transferred to the 91st. After his discharge he returned to Cherry Valley, and to work at his trade. He is an active member of Upton Post, Cherry Valley, where he is now residing with an estimable wife. He has a fine home; here he can be seen after business hours, surrounded by his family, enjoying the fruits of his labor.

POST OFFICERS.

P. W. McIntier,	Commander.
William Southern,	Senior Vice-Commander.
Henry Knox,	Junior Vice-Commander.
Elijah Thurston,	Quartermaster.
Olney Braley,	Adjutant.
	Chaplain.
	Surgeon.
Sedate Foote,	Officer of the Day.
Joshua Weaver,	Officer of the Guard.
David Winton,	Quartermaster Sergeant.

PAST COMMANDERS.

P. McIntier,	D C. Winton,	Thomas Quinby.
W. T. Clinton,	Wm. Southern,	Olney Braley.

LIST OF MEMBERS.

Ackerman, George	F, 121 N. Y.
Bridges, N	G, 3 N. Y. C.
Butler, Edwin	I, 121 N. Y.
Bunnell, Hyatt	C, 152 N. Y.
Blakeley, Andrew	G, 40 N. Y.
Benjamin, W. L	Unknown
Briggs, Lewis C	K, 152 N. Y.
Ballard, George	D, 10 N. Y. A.
Braley, Olney	E, 2nd H. A.
Bishop, Chas. H	C, 152 N. Y.
Carr, Edwin	H, 169 N. Y.
Curtis, Chas. W	F, 15 Ill.
Crawford, Lewis	E, 89 N. Y.
Cummings, Wm. A	I, 8 N. Y. C.
Card, Stephen V	E, 2nd N. Y. H. A.
Cooper, A I	D, 114 N. Y.
Collier, Edwin	D, 61 N. Y.

Cleveland, Harmond............................G, 134 N. Y.
Chase, John...................................G, 2 N. Y. H. A.
Davis, Judson K.............................. 152 N. Y.
Daniels, John N..............................C, 152 N. Y.
Eldred, Edward...............................E, 65 N. Y.
Edwards, W...................................I, 121 N. Y.
Fuller, Albert...............................F, 104 N. Y.
Ferris, Aaron................................H, 151 N.Y.
Foote, Sedate................................I, 121 N. Y.
Genung, Burdett..............................I, 121 N. Y.
Gifford, D. M................................H, 152 N. Y.
Grant, George................................K, 161 N. Y.
Griffin, Richard H...........................I, 46 N. Y,
Green, John W................................G, 7 N. Y. C.
Hall, A. L...................................C, 152 N. Y.
Hargraves, James.............................C, 45 N. L.
Herrick, E. C................................H, 144 N. Y.
Harrington, Marshall.........................C, 90 N. Y,
Jackson, D D.................................K, 121 N, Y.
Knox, Henry.................................. 20 N. Y C.
Kanavan, James...............................C. 8 N Y. C.
Leonard, Frank E., 1st. Lieut................C, 152 N. Y.
Lunn, William................................K, 121 N. Y.
Monroe, Hiram................................C, 152 N. Y.
McIntier, P. W...............................I, 121 N. Y.
Martin, Nelson...............................E, 121 N. Y,
McIntier, Ansel..............................M, 2 N. Y. A,
Moffatt, Wesley C............................E, 69 N. Y.
Mills, Stephen...............................G, 22 N. Y. H. A.
Mattice, Martin V............................G, 2 N. Y. H. A.
Mathers, Elias C.............................K, 121 N. Y.
Nichols Chas.................................G, 121 N. Y.
Ostrander, Edward............................I, 121 N. Y.
Pope, Charles L..............................K, 6 Pa R. C.
Place, R. D..................................C, 152 N. Y.

Quimby, Thorn..................................C, 122 N. Y.
Radley, James..................................H, 152 N. Y.
Robinson, James................................C, 152 N. Y.
Richardson, Geo................................A, 18 N. Y. A.
Southern W. A..................................C, 152 N. Y.
Swart Wm M.....................................K, 121 N. Y.
Swart, A. E....................................I, 20 N. Y. C.
Schuder, Edwin L...............................C, 152 N. Y.
Southern, James................................C, 152 N. Y.
Thayer, Nelson.................................L, 114 N. Y.
Talbut, Orney J................................K, 121 N. Y.
Turner, Andrew.................................A, 1st N. Y. C.
Turner, Andrew.................................A, 1st N. Y. C.
Thurston. Elijah...............................C, 152 N. Y.
Winton, D. C. (Band)...........................51 Regt.
Wood, Erastus..................................K, 2nd N. Y. A.
Weaver, Joshua.................................H, 152 N. Y.
Wormwood, O. B.................................L, 3rd N. Y. H. A.

In Memoriam.

Goodrich, M. D.................................B, 115 N. Y
Graves, Geo. W.................................E, 2nd N. Y. H. A.
Hopkins, A. C..................................D, 33 Iowa V.
Jaquish, E. R..................................I, 127 N. Y.
Pope, Charles L................................H, 6 Penn. R. V. C.
Tuller, D. M...................................H, 152 N. Y.

Graves Decorated by Kidder Post.

Atwell, A .... C, 152 N. Y.
Adams, W. O .... 7 N. Y. C.
Babcock, Adelbert .... H, 121 N. Y.
Barber, Harom .... Record Unknown
Babcock, Henry .... "   "
Bennett, Richard .... I, 121 N. Y.
Bancroft, Jay .... I, 121 N. Y.
Brown, Andrew .... C, 152 N. Y.
Bean, James .... L, 121 N. Y.
Colburn, E B .... C, 152 N. Y.
Card, Abel W .... C, 152 N. Y.
Coltons, Chauncey .... I, 121 N. Y.
Camp, Charles .... I, 121 N. Y.
Camp, Nelson .... I, 121 N. Y.
Chase, Albert .... K, 121 N. Y.
Cummings, Harlon .... K, 7 Mich. Cav.
Chapinsting, Wm .... K, 121 N. Y
Davies, George L .... G, 152 N. Y.
Decker, Jacob .... C, 144 N. Y.
Duroe, Horatio .... K, 121 N. Y.
Elliott, William .... K, 121 N. Y.
Eldridge, Adelbert, ... C. 152 N. Y.
Eronson, Thomas .... K, 121 N Y.
Edwards, Lieut. John, ... B, 121 N. Y.
Elliott, Andrew, ... Record unknown
Fuller, M. D .... H, 152 N. Y.
Fenton, Robert, ... 1 N. Y. Art.
Foot, Zephemah, ... I, 121 N. Y.

Fitch, Isaac..................K, 121 N. Y.
Fenton, Samuel..............I, 121 N. Y.
Fero, Lewis E................F, 114, N Y.
Goodrich, Menze D..........115 N. Y.
Gardner, Freland............2nd N. Y. A.
Goodrich, Alexis.............176 N. Y.
Green, William E...........2nd N. Y. A
Houghtaling, Abram B......A, 1st N. Y. A
Harrington, William........H, 152 N Y.
Hopkins, Abram.............33 Iowa
Hay, James D................134 N. Y. V.
Hitchcock, Charles H......C. 152 N. Y.
Hulburt, Edgar..............114 N. Y.
Hoag, Ransom...............K, 121 N. Y.
Jackson, Wallace W........F, 114 N. Y.
Johnson, Samuel............K, 121 N. Y.
James, Nelson...............Record unknown
Johnson Luther.............,89 N. Y.
Jaquish, Erastus R..........Rec unknown
Kelsey, Chauncey...........C. 152 N Y.
Kirkland, Willard...........C, 152 N. Y.
Kelsey, James...............Rec. unknown
Kidder, Geo. Lieut..........C. 152 N Y.
Kinnee, Alvin................C. 152 N. Y.
Kenyon, Chas L.............U. S. N.
Kinnee, O. P.................C, 152 N. Y.
Lewis, Edwin................I, 121 N. Y.
Lewis, Henry................I, 121 N. Y.
Lewis, David H.............Rec. unknown
Miller, Daniel...............C, 152 N. Y.

McIntier, Levi..Rec. unknown
Miller, James A...C, 152 N. Y.
McClintonteock, E., Sergeent..................Rec. unknown
Marr, Henry.. H, 152 N. Y.
Petingall, Charles .... I, 121 N. Y.
Petingall, E..K, 121 N. Y
Pearsall, Edward W..................................2nd N. Y. A.
Potter, Philip..I, 121 N. Y.
Parcell, Aaron A.. 176 N. Y.
Rhames, William ....Rec. unkown
Ripley, F. A...C, 152 N. Y.
Rockwell, Clark..K, 121 N. Y.
Rexford, Sylvester.. 76 N. Y.
Rotch, Francis M., Col............................. Gov's Staff
Reeves, George.. C, 152 N. Y.
Rogers, Henry.....................................E, 2 N. Y A.
Radley, John ....C, 152 N. Y.
Sergant, Stanley G..................................C, 152 N. Y.
Schism Andrew...H, 121 N. Y.
Simmons, James...K, 121 N. Y.
Scudder, John L.. 20 N. Y.
Snedeker, Garret... 176 N. Y.
Shames, William............................... Rec. unknown
Stockwell, Henry...   "   "
Smith, Albert D...F, 114 N. Y.
Turbush, Clark... 147 N. Y.
Tracy, Henry..I, 121 N. Y.
Wright, Moses...I, 121 N. Y.
Wilson, George Y...C, 152 N. Y.
Whitford, Horatio.......................................K, 121 N. Y.

KENYON HOUSE,

M. M. BISHOP, - Proprietor,

MORRIS, - New York.

FIRST-CLASS IN EVERY RESPECT.

The Table, under the personal suprrvision of Mrs Bisnop contains all the delicacies of the season.

FINE SAMPLE ROOM. —‡— GOOD BAR.

Accommodations for Both Man and Beast.

D. I. LAURENCE,

MAIN STREET, - MORRIS, N. Y.,

Wishes to thank the Old Comrades and Citizens of Morris for their liberal patronage in the past, and to say that he is still on hand with a
—fine stock of—

CHOICE GROCERIES,

DRUGS, MEDICINES,
BOOKS, STATIONERY,
FINE CONFECTIONS, &c.,
TO SELL AT REASONABLE PRICES.

Weldon Post, No. 256,

RICHFIELD SPRINGS, N. Y.

Regular Meetings every Saturday of each month, at G. A. R Hall.

THIS POST was organized, charter received, and mustered into the Department of New York, January 14, 1882, by Mustering Officer Andrew Davidson, assisted by comrades from the Lewis C. Turner Post, of Cooperstown, N. Y.

At the first meeting held by its members P. D. Fay was elected Commander, serving three months, when he resigned and I. D. Peckham was chosen Commander to serve during his unexpired term.

The Post was named in honor of Lieut. Thomas F. Weldon, born at Little Falls in 1839. He enlisted as a private in the 39th New York State Militia, Oct. 21, 1861, and joined the 76th Regt. at the consolidation of the two regiments at Albany, May 1, 1863. He was promoted to 2d Lieut., and Nov. 1st, 1862, was again promoted to 1st Lieut. and assigned to Co. C, which office he held at the time of his death. He won his promotions by good conduct and brave deeds. Wounded at Bull Run, Aug. 29, 1862, and at the battle of Chancellorsville, May, 1863, he was taken prisoner, and for four weeks remained in rebel hands, when he was exchanged, and reached his regiment just in time to take part in the battle of Gettysburg, where he was again wounded. When the Union forces crossed the Rapidan in May, 1864, Lieut. Weldon was at his post, and remained with his comrades through the memorable campaign from the Rapidan to Petersburg, until he was instantly killed at Welden Railroad, Aug. 24, 1864. Death sealed the glorious record of a brave soldier, a true friend and patriot.

I. D. Peckham was chosen Commander for the unexpired term of P. D. Fay, serving from March, 1862, to January, 1863. He enlisted as a private in Co. K, 136th N. Y. V., Aug. 26, 1862, proceeding to the front at once. Participated in the battles of Gettysburg from July 1st to 4th, '63, was captured July 20, '63, by Mosby's cavalry near Goose Creek; was taken to Libby Prison and transferred to Belle Isle; left Belle Isle Sept. 21, and arrived at Annapolis Sept. 24. He was a brave soldier, with undaunted courage, always at his post, amidst the thickest of the fight. He was discharged June 13, 1865, and at the present time is one of the most prominent business men and respected citizens of Richfield Springs.

Richard Weldon was born in Little Falls, Herkimer county, in May, 1839. His parents moved to Richfield Springs when he was three years old, from which place he enlisted, Nov. 3, 1861, in Co. D, Bedan's 1st Regiment U. S. Sharpshooters. Was mustered into the service at Utica, N. Y., going to Washington to Camp Construction, where he remained until spring. While there he contracted measles, and was sent to the Indiana Hospital, Patent Office, Washington, where he remained from January to March, 1862. When he joined his regiment he was ordered to Arlington Heights, Va., and down the Potomac to Hampton, thence to Big Bethel, engaging in the battles at Big and Little Bethel; thence to and participating in the seige of Yorktown; thence up the Pamonka river to Gaines' Mills, remaining about two months, and while there went up to and fought in the battle at Hanover Court House, after which he returned to Gaines' Mills, arriving there about two days before the battle of Fair Oaks, and was doing picket duty there when the seven days' fight commenced. As long as time shall last the glorious record of this famous regiment will be remembered as one of the coolest, bravest and most daring of the army. Participating in all the battles, skirmishes and marches of the regiment from the time he enlisted until discharged at Harrison Landing, Aug. 7, he is justly entitled to its honors. He returned to Richfield Springs after the war, and upon the organization of the Post he was elected Sen. Vice Commander, which office he held until he was elected Commander for 1891. His administration was in keeping with the sturdy manliness which he is known to possess. The exercises on May 30, 1888, (Decoration Day), during his term as Commander, was one of the most imposing since the Post was organized, comrades being present from Cooperstown, Brookfield and Springfield. Commander Weldon was Capt. Co. E, 9th N. Y. N. G.; was charter member of H. & L. Co. No. 1, Richfield Springs; Asst. Foreman for three, and Foreman for two years. Now residing with his family, wife, three sons and five daughters at Richfield Springs, N. Y.

Allen W. Denison, the present Commander, was born at Warren, Herkimer Co., N Y., completing his education at Richfield Springs; accepted a clerkship at Utica, N. Y., from which place he enlisted as a private in Co. E, 14th N. Y. V., on the 17th of May, 1861; mustered in at Albany, going from here to New York, thence to Washington, and to Halls Hill. On the 1st of July crossed the Potomac and into Virginia; took charge of Ferry, Acqueduct and Fort McQuade, remaining here until spring of

1862; was ruptured while here, sent to Seminary Branch Hospital, Georgetown; was discharged from here in April 1862, and returned to Morris, where he has since resided. Joined Weldon Post, was elected Sen. Vice for three years and Commander to serve during 1888. His administration of the Post's affairs was one of the most successful since it was organized, and he was again called into active service by being elected Commander for 1892. Has served as Assessor of the town of Warren for six years, Deputy Sheriff of County for six years, and Collector for one year. He is now residing in town of Warren, near Richfield, his family consisting of self and an estimable wife.

Edwin B. Wilcox was born in Oneida Co., going to Madison Co. when five years old. Was educated at Clarksville Academy; leaving school, he learned the carpenter trade: enlisted Aug. 14, 1861, as private in Co. A, 1st N. Y. Lt. Artillery; was engaged in the battle of Fair Oaks, discharged Oct. 1862, re-enlisted at Grand Rapids, Mich., and recruited Co. D. for the 10th Mich. Cavalry, and was commissioned by Gov. Crapo as Captain of said Company in Jan. 1863. He did splendid service in the field at the battles of Lookout Mountain, Pea Ridge, Stony Creek, Rawley, N. C., and Strawberry Plains. Was detailed, and placed on the Staff of Gen. Upton, and afterwards on the Staffs of Gen. Gillmore and Gen. Stoneman in the Ordinance Department at Knoxville, Tenn. While here, he was ordered to his regiment at Memphis, in Nov. 1865, to be discharged. In 1872, he removed to Richfield Sprg's. Is charter member of Post, and has served as Quartermaster, Chaplain, and Junior Vice Commander.

Peter W. Tallman was born at Schuyler, Herkimer Co., N. Y.; after leaving school he learned the carpenter trade: enlisted Aug. 28, 1862, as a private in Co. E, 152nd

Reg. N. Y. V.; mustered into the U. S. service at Camp Schuyler, going to the front at Chain Bridge, and thence to Washington. The record of this regiment is his record, Always on duty, meeting the foe at the Wilderness, fighting them until the surrender of Lee at Appomattox, engaging in twenty-two battles, and discharged. Returned to the town of Schuyler in 1878, and then moved to Richfield Springs. Is a charter member, and has served as Sergeant-Major, Junior and Senior Vice of Weldon Post, and was elected President of the 152d Regiment Association for 1892.

Luzerne B. Wheeler, born in Otsego county in July, 1827, enlisting at Richfield Springs in August, 1862, as private in Co. B, 152d N. Y. V., going to Chain Bridge, and from there to the defense of Washington. Was all through Longstreet's siege, and with Grant in the Wilderness, participating in the battles of Suffolk and the Peninsula, the Wilderness, (including the seven days' fight) and at Spotsylvania. Was taken sick at Spotsylvania and sent to the hospital. He is a charter member of Weldon Post, and has served as Senior and Junion Vice Commander, and Officer of the Day.

Tremain I. Jaques was born in Oneida Co., in Aug., 1834, going to Richfield Springs when only four years old. He enlisted August 30th, 1862, as a recruit for Battery M, 3d N. Y. L. A., (formerly the 19th Infantry), and in October, 1862, was ordered to New York; thence to Hatteras, N. C., where he joined his regiment, Nov. 1st, 1862, his company at the time being at New Berne, and on Feb'y 3d, 1863, he was sent to his company. Engaged in battle at New Berne, and remained, doing guard duty until the fall of 1863. Ordered to Norfolk and to Getty's Station for winter quarters. In March, 1864, he went to Great Bridge in the Dismal Swamp, N. C., and from there to

F. M. FIRMAN,

DEALER IN

Fine Groceries & Canned Goods,

Vegetables and all kinds of Farm Produce,

✦ FISH AND OYSTERS ✦

In their Season.

Centre Street,

(Three doors below 1st Nat. Bank,)

Richfield Springs, N. Y.

BOOK SELLER
AND
STATIONER.

WALL PAPER
FINE CHINA, FANCY GOODS, &c.
✦ ✦ ✦ ✦ ✦

L. L. Brockway,

GLADSTONE
BLOCK,

RICHFIELD SPRINGS.
NEW YORK.

Newport News, thence to Yorktown and to Hampton, Va., and aboard boats up the James River to City Point, Wilson Landing and Fort Powhattan, and engaged in battle with Gen. Lee; thence to Bermuda Hundred, across Point of Rocks, on the Appomattox; thence to near Petersburg, and was under fire from June 22 to August 24; ordered to outside of entrenchments of Richmond, near Dutch Gap, for winter; March, 1864, crossed the James River, engaged in artillery and cavalry fight; then in battle at Fort Harrison on the banks of the James River, and after battle back to camp. Received marching orders on the night of the 2d of April, 1865, and entered Richmond with the 24th Corps at 3 a. m.; guarded the city until June 27th, 1865, and was then discharged. Returned to Richfield Springs, joined Weldon Post, and was elected Commander, serving with distinction, and is now serving as adjutant.

POST OFFICERS.

A. W. Denison,......................Commander.
Joseph Eagan,...................... Senior Vice-Commander.
Alfred Barker, ... Junior Vice-Commander.
Tremain I. Jaques,............... Adjutant.
I. D. Peckham,........, ...Quartermaster.
W. B. Crain,......... ....Surgeon.
John Burgess,......................Chaplain.
Luzerne Wheeler,............. ... Officer of the Day.
Oliver Carson,......................Officer of the Guard.
John Depne,........................Sergeant-Major.
R. Weldon,........................Quartermaster Sergeant.

PAST COMMANDERS.

P. D. Fay,	I. D. Peckham,	Harmon House,
	Tremain I. Jaques.	
W. A. Swift.	A. W. Dennison.	Richard Wilson.

List of Members.

Allan, A.	D, 152 N. Y.
Anderson, Philander	E, 14 N. Y.
Allen, David	K, 2 N. Y. C.
Ames, John S.	122 N. Y.
Brownrigg, William	K, 1 N. Y. A.
Burgiss, John	Not known.
Barker, Alfred	F, 184 N. Y.
Balch, Delos	G, 1 H. A.
Caldwell, Henry	121 N. Y.
Carson, Oliver	L, 2 N. Y. C.
Crain, W. B.	Asst. Surgeon, 2 Md.
Dutcher, Winnie	F, 16 N. Y. H. A.
Dingman, William	G, 18 Vet Res.
Denison, A. W.	F, 14 N. Y.
Davis, Norman	B, 101 N. Y.
Depue, **John**	F, 134 N. Y.
Eason, Henry O	E, 24 Vet. Res.
Egan, Joseph	Not known
Fay, Parker D.	152 N. Y.
Failey, Patrick	G, 117 N. Y.
Fairchild, Lewis D.	B, 2 Mich. H. A.
Failing, John	M, 1 N. Y. C.
Fiske, Charles	16 N. Y. H. A.
Goodrich, **W. H.**	H, 44 N. Y.
Green, George	152 N. Y.
House, Harmon	G, 152 N. Y.
Hyde, Charles	B, 1 N. Y. A.; 22 Penn. Res.
Hammond, A.	F, 34 N. Y.
Haight, Orin	121 N. Y.
Handy, **David**	Bat. M, 3 N. Y. L. A.
Jaques, Tremain I.	Bat. M, 3 N. Y. L. A.
Knocks, John	D, 2 U. S. Mtd Art.
Kenyon, S. P.	U. S. Mtd Inf.

Lippins, John E...U. S. N.
Mason, James A.............................. ...F, 1 Ind. Bat.
Niles, Ceylon..G, 1 N. Y. C.
Osterhout, Justin..................................16 N Y. H. A.
Peckham, I. D.................. ....K, 136 N. Y.
Swift, W. A...F, 1 N. Y. C.
Sporburg Edward.......................................121 N. Y.
Scramlin, Charles........................D, 16 Iowa Vet. Vol.
Taylor Carson P ....G, 2 N Y. Mtd. Vol.
Tallman, Peter W..E, 152 N. Y.
Wheeler, Luzerne.. B, 152 N. Y.
Weldon, Thomas.......................... E. 16 N. Y. H. A.
Wilcox, E. B.................Co. D. 10 Mich. Cav.; A, 1 N. Y. Art
Weldon, Richard...........................D, 1 U. S. S S.
West, Milton P...K, 2 N. Y.
Wood, Jerome A ....G, 6 N. Y. C.
Wood, H. H........................... ....G, N. Y. Mtd. Vol.
Warmley, Henry J. ....G, N. Y. C.
Young, Elias..152 N. Y.
Zotler, Burton................................ ....B, 14 N. Y.

ELIAS YOUNG CAMP, S. OF V., 112.

Richfield Springs, N. Y.

At a meeting held in the G. A. R. rooms, Dec. 2, 1890, this Camp was orgamized and mustered in by Comrade Fisher, Chief Mustering Officer. Geo. W. Hyde was elected Captain; Williams Kingsley, 1st Lieut., and Ralph Barren, 2d Lieut. When the change was made as to the titles of officers, William Kingsley was elected Commander, Joseph L. Boardman, Senior Vice, and Mortimer Wires, Junior Vice Commander. Among the members of this Camp are the most prominent young men in Richfield Springs. Under the administration of Commander Kingsley the Camp is in most excellent shape and its membership steadily increasing.

LIST OF MEMBERS.

G. W. Hyde, William Kingsley. George A. Peckham, R. G. Seamons, William Carson, Jesse Burgess, Fred. Shellman, James F. Weldon, M. Wires, J. L. Boardman, G. W. Sporburg, E. R. Wilcox, Jr., Charles E. Teabout, Daniel Henderson, John W. Swift, Myron Barker, Elnor Sporburg, W. T. Weldon, William Hellinus, Ralph Barnes.

E. D. Farmer Post, No. 119,

ONEONTA, N. Y.

Regular Meetings every Tuesday Evening at G. A. R Hall.

THIS POST was organized and mustered into the Department of New York, Jan. 21, 1871, by Mustering Officer, General John C. Robinson, of Watrous Post, No. 30, of Binghamton, N. Y., assisted by comrades from that Post. Since its organization in 1871, there has been mustered into the Post and received by card, 215 members; this number has been reduced by death and various other causes, until there are but 85 members left.

The Post was named in honor of one of Oneonta's worthy sons, Edwin D. Farmer, a brother of the worthy ex-President of the W. R. C., Miss Eliza Farmer. He was a brave soldier, whose name will forever remain on the roll of honor, without spot or blemish to mar its purity. Born at Oneonta in 1834, and in August, 1863, enlisted as a private in Co. K, 121 N. Y. V., serving with his regiment (the record of which is written in this volume) with great courage and devotion, until he was killed at the battle of Chancellorsville, showing in battle the same fearlessness and uncompromising fortitude that had distinguished his life. He was a most exemplary man—a model soldier.

"Went forth to the field of conflict,
   Fought bravely our loved land to save,

Gave up his life in the service.
And now sleeps in an unknown grave."

James Roberts, Past Commander, was born at Westfield, Otsego county, N. Y., in June, 1827. He received a commom school education. After leaving school he worked on a farm until he became of age, taking up his residence at Oneonta, and going into the grocery business in 1859. The war had broken out, and the loyal people of the North were responding nobly to each and every call for troops. The gallant Farragut had cut in twain the Confederacy, and Grant had achieved glorious and and brilliant victories in the West. Dupont and Burnside had also gained substantial victories, and Worden, with his Monitor was monarch of the seas. These great victories, decisive as they were, had been partially overcome by the failure of the campaign in the Peninsula, and the nation was tingling under the shadow of the seven days' battle. The President had called for 500,000 volunteers, and in response to that call Comrade Roberts left friends and the pleasurers of home, entrusting his business to the charge of an employe, enlisted, Aug. 11. 1862, as a private in Co. G, 3d N. Y. C. He participated in the battles at Kingston, N. C., White Hall and Goldsborough. After the battle of Goldsborough he went to Newport News for winter quarters. In February was ordered back to North Carolina ; thence to Portsmouth, doing duty in the Dismal Swamp, Great Bridge and Suffolk ; crossed the "black water" and in the battle at Stony Creek, May 7, 1864, and Notaway Bridge, May 8 ; thence to City Point and Bermuda Hundred, dismounting and for some time doing duty between the Appomattox and James Rivers ; recrossed the Appomattox, doing duty on the left of the army in front of Petersburg ; crossing to the north side of the James, remaining there until the fall of 1864, and to Portsmouth for winter quarters; thence to Norfolk to guard duty, and was discharged June 11, 1865, and returned to Oneonta. He can refer with pride to his record—that of his regiment. He engaged in the battles of White Hall, Goldsborough, Dec. 16 and 17, Jacksonville, Jan. 15, Trenton, July 20, Bottom Bridge, Feb. 7, Stony Creek, May 7, Notaway Bridge, May 8, Black and White, May 14, before Petersburg, June 16, Ream's Station, June 29, and Prince George Court House, Sept. 15, 1864. He is a charter member of Farmer Post, and served one year as Senior Vice. Was Mustering Officer of Hill Post, at Laurens, and assisted in the organization of the Post, at Schenevus, Delhi and Milford. His administration as Commander was noted for promptness, discipline and sociability. Has served as collector for the town of Oneonta for four years, town clerk for three years, and village trustee for one year. Enlisting as a private, was promoted to corporal. The commissary of the regiment had obtained a furlough, and while North, died. Roberts, who had been acting Commissary, was, in July, 1864, placed on the Colonel's staff, and promoted to Commissary of the Regiment.

H. C. Whitman, born at West Oneonta, Otsego county, N. Y., Oct. 6, 1841; attended the district school until 15 years old, completing his education at the Gilbertsville Academy in 1858, and going on a farm. He enlisted Sept. 9, 1863, at Albany, N. Y., as a recruit for the 3d N. Y. Cavalry; left Albany same night for Park Barracks, New York, and twenty-four hours after ordered to Fort Hamilton to wait transportation.; left Fort Hamilton with other recruits, Sept. 22, by government transports, for New Berne, N. C., experiencing a rough voyage, especially while passing, and in the vicinity of Hatteras Inlet, entering the bay, and up the Neuse river to New Berne; joined the regiment Sept. 28, and was assigned to

Co. G, receiving horses and equipments, and was an active participant in the great drama. The members of this gallant regiment can refer with pride to the many battles in which they acquitted themselves with honor: At Williamson, Kingston, White Hall, Goldsborough, Trenton, Sandy Ridge, Tarboro, Warsaw, Streets Ferry, Stony Creek, Notaway Bridge, Black and White, before Petersburg, Jan. 15, 1864, Ream's Station, Malvern Hill, Prince George Court House, Johnson's Farm, Sept. 29 and Oct. 7, and at Charles City Pike, Oct. 20, 1864. Was discharged at Suffolk, Va., June 7, 1865. Returned to Oneonta and joined E. D. Farmer Post; was Senior Vice during 1885, and Commander for the year 1886. During his term of office, in the latter part of May, the Post was presented with a beautiful silk flag by the ladies of Oneonta. His administration was conducted on business principles, and he surrendered his office to his successor, Comrade Butts, the rooster showing an increase in the membership during his term. He served as justice of the peace for four years, from 1885 to 1889. He is a prominent Mason, a member of the Blue Lodge and Chapter, of Oneonta, N. Y. He is now residing with his family—an estimable wife, two sons and a daughter, ages, 22, 11 and 9—at 17 Cedar street, Oneonta, N. Y., and is employed as a traveling salesman, in the employ of Luzerne Westcott.

A. M. Barnes, Commander for the years 1882-83, was born in Maryland in August, 1839. When twelve years old he went to Cobleskill, completing his education, and going on a farm; taught school for two terms; enlisted in Aug., 1862, in Co. H., 152 N. Y. V.; was ordered to the defence of Washington, on the Virginia side, doing guard duty; was at the seige of Suffolk, April 11 to May 3, 1863. His record is that of his regiment, participating in its battles and skirmishes; was wounded at the battle of North Ann River, sent to Mt. Pleasant hospital, and one month afterward sent to Davids Island, N. Y. Discharged, Jan. 13, 1865. Returned to Cobleskill and moved to Oneonta in 1875, engaging in the furniture and undertaking business.

Robert Winn, born at Otego, N. Y., February 7, 1835, and attended the common school at that place. Moved to Oneonta in 1847, going on a farm. He enlisted Aug. 8, 1862, in Co. G., 3 N. N. C.; mustered in at Albany, and ordered to New Berne, N. C. He was a good soldier and did splendid service with a fighting regiment. The record of the regiment is his record—engaged in eighteen hard-fought battles, which are given in the record of other comrades of Farmer Post. Discharged June 25, 1865. Returned to Oneonta, joining Farmer Post, and elected Commander for 1890.

J. M. Ellis, born in Schoharie county in 1884; was educated at that place, and engaged in farming. He enlisted Dec. 25, 1863, as a private in Co. E, 13 N. Y. H. A. Was mustered in at Schenectady, N. Y., in Jan., 1864; ordered to Portsmouth, Va., and Getty's Station; sent to the hospital for general disability, and discharged in Sept., 1885. Returned to Schoharie, and in 1866 moved to Oneonta; joined Farmer Post in August, 1888; has served as Surgeon and Junior Vice Commander, and is present Officer of the Day.

Edwin G. Bixby, born the 23d day of November, 1845, at Newport, Ohio; when four years old moved to Davenport, Delaware county, N. Y.; attended the district school, completing his education at the Syracuse, N. Y., Business College. After leaving school he learned the mason and bricklayer trade. August 15, 1864, he enlisted at Norwich, N. Y., as a private in Co. G, 5th N. Y. Heavy Art., and was mustered into the U. S. service Aug. 16, 1865, at the same place; was ordered to report at Harper's Ferry, and joined his regiment at Berryville, West Virginia, in the Shanendoah Valley, participating in the battle of Winchester, Sept. 19, 1864, (Phil. Sheridan's first fight), and Fisher's Hill, Sept. 22, 1864. While on a reconnaisance, was wounded at Cedar Creek, Oct. 13, 1864, and sent to hospital at Baltimore and to Philadelphia. Discharged from hospital in February, 1865, and started for the front to join his regiment, when he was taken with small-pox and sent to small-pox hospital, Feb. 14, 1865, remaining there until April, 1865. Was discharged from service June 25th, at Alexandria. Returned to Delaware county, and in April, 1866, removed to Oneonta, and is at the present time a member of the firm of Jennings & Bixby, plumbers and gas fitters. He is a charter member of E. D. Farmer Post; served as Senior Vice for one year, and elected Commander for the year 1883. The Post, at the commencement of his term of office, having scarcely enough members to hold their charter, the outlook at this time was anything but promising, but Commander Bixby had accepted the trust, and realizeng the situation and what was expected of him, he lost no time, but set out at once to make an effort to place the Post on a better footing in the department. The members of Farmer Post had made no mistake in select- a Commander for ihis work. He proved an exceedingly popular officer, and his administration of the Post's affairs was in keeping with the sturdy manliness which he is known to possess, acting always with a strict adherence to the adage, "What is worth doing at all, is worth doing well." He surrendered his office at the end of his term, the Post having forty members in good standing. He had put new life into the organization, and renewed energy to its members. He was a delegate to the State encampment for four years; also on the Department Staff, as Aide de Camp to Commander Floyd Clarkson. He was a delegate to the convention at Albany, when a committee was appointed to take the first steps looking to the building of a Soldiers' Home. It was his pleasure afterwards to witness the laying of the corner-stone, and to be present at its dedication, as a delegate from E. D. Farmer Post, on both occasions.

Peter Weidman was born at Berne, Albany county, N. Y., August 7, 1829, and when ten years old went to Unadilla, Otsego, county, where he received a common school education. On leaving school he learned the painter's trade. When the rebellion had assumed such gigantic proportions, and the President had, in July, 1864, called for 500,000 volunteers, he deemed it his duty to sacrifice everything dear to his heart at home, to aid in crushing the rebellion, and enlisted as a recruit for Co. H, 144th Regiment, under Captain Siver. Was with his regiment, engaging in all its battles and skirmishes, enduring its hardships and sharing its honors, until he was discharged by special order No. 282, June 17, 1865, on account of sickness in his family, the regiment being discharged three weeks later. He returned to Unadilla, where he worked at his trade. Was a charter member of C. C. Siver Post, and served as Quartermaster. Removing to Oneonta, he joined the E. D. Farmer Post, 119, of Oneonta, by transfer card from Siver Post, in 1883, was soon after elected Junior Vice Commander and Senior Vice, and was elected Post Commander to serve during the year. He was an exceedingly popular officer, of genial disposition, and a social companion. Faithful and true as he was to the cause for which he offered his services, he has at all times and on all occasions when opportunity offered, been just as true to the Society, and quick to honor the men whose patriotism led them to throw their lives into the scale against treason, and his interest has been just as keen to perpetuate and strengthen that noble order, which has maintained, and through the Sons of Veterans and Sons of Sons of Veterans, etc., will forever maintain and seal the principles for which they fought. When the Sons of Veterans Camp at Oneonta was organized, it was mustered in as the Peter Weidman Camp, Sons of Veterans, in honor of the subject of this brief sketch. Comrade Weidman presenting to the Sons of Veterans a beautiful silk flag. He has been village trustee for six years, is a member of the Ancient Order of United Workmen, and a prominent member of the Order of Red Men. He is now residing in Oneonta, 63 Church street, his wife being a member of Woman's Relief Corps.

Among the names of the most substantial business men of Oneonta, who are members of Farmer Post, is that of W. H. Morris. He was born at Milford in July, 1841, receiving a common school education at that place, and after leaving school going on a farm. He enlisted as a private in Co. G, 1st N. Y. Eng., Oct. 1, 1861, and was mustered into the service Oct. 3, 1861, at New York city. Was ordered to Staten Island and thence to the Department at Hilton Head; was discharged at New York in December, 1864. He returned to Milford, and in May, 1865, removed to Oneonta, engaging in the cigar and tobacco business and in the same year embarked in the hotel business. He became associated, in 1867, with his brother, Albert H., in the wholesale flour and feed business at Oneonta, where he is located at the present writing, doing an extensive business, their trade covering a a large territory adjacent to Oneonta. Is a charter member of the Post, but his extensive business require his personal attention and time to such an extent that he refuses to accept an office at the hands of the Post. He retains a deep interest in its welfare, and no important matter coming before the Post is finally concluded without receiving the benefit of his counsel and advice. He is President of the State Normal School Board, of Oneonta. He was Supervisor of the town during the years 1880-81, trustee of the village, a prominent Mason and Knights Templar, and an honored and respected citizen.

W. A Southworth was born in Otego county, August 26, 1843. He completed his education at the Kingston Academy in 1861, and enlisted July 11, 1862, in Co. A, 114th N. Y. V., and was mustered in at Binghamton, Sept. 23, 1862, going to Baltimore, and discharged June 1, 1863, by reason of general disability. Reinlisted Jan. 11, 1864, in Co. E, 89th N. Y. V., as a recruit, joining his regiment at Folly Island, S. C, in March, 1864. His record is that of his regiment. Discharged Aug. 5, 1865. Joined C. C. Siver Post, and in 1885 joined E. D. Farmer Post. He served as Officer of the Day, Senior Vice, and was elected Commander for the year 1891. During his administration he originated the idea of an open meeting each month, when the G. A. R., S. of V. and the W. R. C. meet together with invited friends. These meetings are well attended and much enjoyed by the members of the different societies.

M. D. Munson was born at Davenport, Delaware county, N. Y., July 24, 1841, and was educated at the common schools, then going on a farm. He enlisted in August, and was mustered into the service, Sept. 2, 1864, as a private in Company D, 144th N. Y. V., going to Hilton Head, S. C.; was in the hospital from October to December,

1864. His record is that of his regiment. A brave soldter, always at his post—he is entitled to all the honors due his regiment. Dircharged June 25, 1865. Returned to Davenport, and in 1880 removed to Oneonta. Joined Farmer post in 1882. Has served as clerk of the town of Davenport and treasurer of the village of Oneonta. He is now residing with his family at Oneonta, and is in the employ of J. C. Roberts.

Charles L. Wilbur was born at Davenport, July 7, 1841; was educated at the district school and the Furgison Academy; taught school, and in 1861 commenced reading law in the office of Gen. S. S. Bundy, at Oneonta, N. Y. He enlisted at Davenport in Co. I, 144th N. Y. V., going to Upton Hill, Va. Was injured and sent back to Stanton Hospital, Washington, D. C. Discharged in December, 1852. In July, 1863, entered Abram Becker's office at Furgisonville; going West in 1867, and returning in 1872, and remained until his father died in December, 1875; he then went to Oneonta, and renewed his studies in the office of Gen. Burnside; and was admitted to the bar in January, 1875. He is an active menber of Farmer Post. He was the Democratic candidate for Member of Assembly in the 2d Assembly district of Otsego county in 1891, and was defeated by one of the strongest candidates the Republicans could have nominated, by 600 majority, this district usually giving over 1,000 majority.

Orlon Harmon was born at Binghamton, N. Y., March 24, 1832. He attended the public schools and completed his education at the Business College at Binghamton, where he studied civil engineering. In the spring of 1861 he rented a farm near Binghamton, and was plowing in the field when, in answer to his country's call, he left the plow to rust in the furrow, and went to the city of Binghamton and enlisted under Capt. J. J. Bartlett, a few days after going to Elmira, where, on the 21st day of May, the 27th Regiment, N. Y. V. was organized, and was mustered into the United States service, July 5, 1861, and ordered to Washington July 10th. The regiment was assigned to the First Brigade July 15, 1861, and received orders the same day to march "on to Richmond;" crossed the long bridge over the Potomac, passed out through the fortifications, and on to Baily cross-roads, where they halted for supper: went into camp about 10 p. m. on the Annandale Hills, about twelve miles from Washington; at sunrise was ordered to Fairfax Court House, and July 18 went into camp near Centerville; returned to Washington and remained until August; thence to near Alexandria, and helped to build several forts in the defences of Washington. Near the last of August removed camp to a beautiful elevation south of Hunting Creek, where they built Fort Lyon, one of the strongest forts in the chain of defences surrounding the capital; in January, 1862, was detailed and sent North as a recruiting officer. Rejoined regiment at Yorktown, arriving about a week before its evacuation. May 3d the regiment, then assigned to the Second Brigade, was sent up the York river in pursuit of rebels; landed at West Point, under the thunder of the guns of the war ships. Early the next morning we found the enemy in great force, and was forced back, fighting with considerable loss; by easy marching arrived at White House May 15. McClellan's army made a junction at this point, and after resting, (May 20), moved on toward Richmond, reaching Mechanicsville, May 27th, and three days after the battle of Fair Oaks was fought, and June 24th fought the battle of Seven Pines. June 25, 1862, a series of battles was commenced at Oak Grove, lasting until July 2; July 26 the battle of Mechanicsville was fought, and July 27 the battle Gaines at Mills, a bloody battle, at which he received a gun shot wound in the right breast, the ball passing into his body, and could not be extracted, so is still carried as a memento of the great struggle for Union and Liberty. Two straggling soldiers, one on each side, helped him to Savage Station, on the R. & G. R. railroad, where he went into a large hospital tent. After waiting two hours before a surgeon came to his aid, the surgeon probed his wound with his finger, then gave him an opium pill and a drink of brandy, which he interpreted to mean that the surgeon considered his case hopeless. Assisted by three friends in the civil service from Binghamton, he reached the James River just in time to board the Stepping Stone, which was loading with sick and wounded for Fortress Monroe, where he arrived July 31, four days after the battle. Here his wound was dressed for the first time. Remained there two weeks and was sent to the City Hospital, Brooklyn, where he received splendid care. Rejoined his regiment at Washington, and the next morning started for the Second Bull Run, where they arrived just after Pope's retreat had commenced. Was on Centerville Heights, where Generals Kearney and Stevens were killed at Chantilly on the last day of August, 1862. The whole army fell back within the fortifications around Washington. Broke camp, Sept. 5, crossed the long bridge through Washington, Sept. 14, confronting the enemy at the base of South Mountains, about 4 p. m.; ordered to carry Crampton Pass, which they did, camping that night on the top of the mountains. Sept. 14, off for the greater battle of Antietam. Sept. 18th, General Lee sent a flag of truce, requesting an armistice until 5 p. m. to bury the dead, which Gen. McClellan made a mistake in granting. During that night Lee retreated across the Potomac, taking advantage of the truce of the day before to arrange for the same. October 31st, marched back through Maryland to the Potomac at Berlin, and crossed on pontoons; Nov. 10, arrived at Warrentown, where McClellan was relieved and Burnside placed in command. November 15th, broke camp and started for Fredericksburg, arriving, Dec. 4, at Bell Plain, Burnside's base of operations, for his Fredericksburg campaign; December 10, to White Oak Church, and on the 11th brought up at the Rappahannock, just below the City of Fredericksburg. The Union batteries were placed along the river, opposite and below the city, and shortly after the regiment came up, opened on the place, sending sixty shells a minute, which went crashing into and through the buildings of the city. Jan. 26th, Burnside was relieved and Hooker placed in command; was with Sedgwick in the Sixth Corps during Hooker's campaign. Was mustered out at Elmira, Jan. 4, 1863. Returned to Binghamton and was made an enrolling officer and deputy provost marshall for the 26th district of New York, and helped to consumate the first draft; was appointed a government agent on the military railroads of Virginia under Chief Engineer W. L. Wentz. Locating at Oneonta, he joined Farmer Post and was elected Commander for 1892. He is a most excellent presiding officer, and his administration of its affairs tends to enhance the reputation of the Post.

C. J. Westcott was born, Feb. 4, 1842, at Richmondville, Schoharie county, N. Y.; attended the common school; moved to Westford, thence to Worcester, completing his education at the Worcester Academy; after leaving school went on a farm, leaving the farm and the pleasures of home when his country called for help to share the toils and pains of a soldier's life, enlisting at Worcester, Aug. 23, 1862, and mustered a private in Co. I, 121st N. Y. V., at Herkimer, N. Y., Aug. 27, 1862.

Ordered to the front at once, going to Washington and joining the Army of the Potomac at Crampton Pass; was in the skirmish at Fredericksburg; thence to White Oak Church, where he remained during the winter. He was wounded at the battle of the Wilderness and sent to Finly hospital, Washington; after remaining there two weeks he was granted a furlough for thirty days; rejoined his regiment just before the battle of Cedar Creek. He was with his regiment, participating in all its battles, etc., during its period of service, barring his absence from the regiment by reason of wounds received at the battle of the Wilderness. Among the prominent battles of the regtment are Gettysburg, Rappahonnock Station, Fredericksburg, Salem Heights, Spotsylvania, Cold Harbor and Fisher Hill. Where the fire was hottest and bullets flew thickest, you would find young Wescott. Was discharged at Hall's Hill, Va., June 25, 1865. Returned to Decatur, N. Y., and in 1867 removed to Guilford, Chenango county and engaged in the lumber business; remained there until 1874, when he sold his mill and embarked in the commission business. In 1877 he accepted a position as a commercial traveller, and in 1880 moved to Milford and engaged in the hop business, in the employ of D. Wilbur & Son, where he remained for ten years. Since that time he has been interested in the firm of L. Westcott, real estate and hop dealer. Was a charter member of Post at Guilford, N. Y., and also a charter member of Olcott Post, 522, formerly of Milford, now of Portlandville. Joined E. D. Farmer Post, 119, by card, March 15, 1892. He is an exceedingly popular gentleman among his comrades and friends, and in obtaining his membership Farmer Post adds another substantial business man of Oneonta to their roster.

Orwell A. Benton was born at Sidney, N. Y., in 1843,

completing his education at Brooklyn, Pa., in 1851, and went on a farm. Enlisted Oct. 23, 1863, in Co. D, 146th N. Y. V., and was mustered in as a recruit in October. Was ordered to the front, wounded at Spotsylvania, May 9th, 1864, sent to the field hospital, thence to Baltimore and later to the Germantown hospital, Philadelphia, Pa. Discharged April 5, 1865. Joined Watrous Post, Binghamton, and Farmer Post by card in 1873.

J. C. Richmond was born at Albany, N. Y., in February, 1848. While attending school he enlisted as a private in Co. E, 177th N. Y. V., and was ordered to New Orleans. Participated in the battles at Ponchatula, Port Hudson, Donaldsville, White River and Brazo City. Was discharged at Albany, Sept. 10th, 1853. Re-enlisted, and was assigned to the 2d Dragoons, and soon after transferred to the 6th U. S. Cavalry. Engaged in the battles at Winchester, Sailor Creek, Staunton and many skirmishes. Was captured and sent to Libby Prison, remaining one month, when Grant entered the city. Was paroled and sent to Annapolis, Md. In April, 1865, went to Philadelphia and enlisted in the U. S. Marine Corps. April 14, went to Washington the same hour Lincoln was shot, and placed on guard and in charge of the prisoners in the conspiracy; remained there until they were executed and then went to sea on board the steamer Shanandoah. and around the world, through the East Indies; was in Japan fifteen months, with the American Minister, as orderly sergeant. For distinguished services he was promoted to and discharged as Brevet Second Lieutenant. Returned to Albany in 1875; moved to Oneonta and joined Farmer Post in 1878. He has served as Officer of the Day, as delegate to the National Encampment, and as Commander of the Post.

The history of the Post would be incomplete did we fail to mention the urbane Past Commander, John C. Ingalls, a brave and faithful soldier. He enlisted in Co. G, of the celebrated 3d N. Y. Cavalry, serving with distinction throughout. Whether at White Hall, Goldsborough, Jacksonville, Trenton, Bottom Bridge, Wheeling, Stony Creek, Notaway Bridge, Black and Whites, before Petersburg, at Ream's Station, or at Prince George Court House, he displayed undaunted courage and devotion to duty. Sacred as are the memories of the past, he is one of those who can truly say: "I have seen and participated in a conflict having no paralell since the world began. His administration as commander was in keeping with his splendid service on the field, and he surrendered to his immediate successor, upon the expiration of his term, the affairs of E. D. Farmer Post, ranking second to none in the county. He is now residing in Oneonta with his family, and is employed at the shops of the D. & H. R. R. Co. at that place.

W. B. S. Paul was born at Albany July 2, 1847. After leaving school he accepted a position as a clerk. He enlisted in Co. I, 91st N. Y. V., joining the regiment at Black and Whites Station, near Petersburg; March 1, was ordered to Washington. Was doing guard duty at Petersburg when Lee surrendered. After his discharge he returned to Albany and was employed by the National Express Co.; in 1877 was placed in charge of the Pennsylvania division, with headquarters in Carbondale, and was soon after placed in charge of the office at Oneonta, N. Y., where he is now residing. His family consists of an estimable wife a daughter, now residing at Fort Plain, and a son, James Hatt, now bookkeeper in the Merchants and Mechanics Bank at Carbondale, Pa., and George S., in the office with his father. He joined Farmer Post in

July. 1891, and is at present Officer of the Day. He is also a prominent member of the Royal Arcanum.

POST OFFICERS.

Orlon Harmon, ... Commander.
J. Elliott .... Senior Vice-Commander.
M. Chandler .... Junior Vice-Commander.
E. W. Jaynes .... Quartermaster.
Elias B Swart .... Chaplain.
S. H. Brown .... Adjutant.
P. Weidman .... Surgeon.
John Ellis ... . Officer of the Day.
A. A. Walling .... Officer of the Guard.
W. B S Paul .... Sergeant-Major.
E. G. Bixby .... Quartermaster Sergeant.

PAST COMMANDERS.

R. L. Fox,	E. G. Bixby,	E. Reynolds,
J. C. Ingalls,	James Roberts,	A. W. Barnes,
H. C. Whitman,	E. L. Butts,	Peter Weidman,
C. A Potter,	Robert Winn.	J. C. Richmond,

William P. Southworth.

LIST OF MEMBERS.

Allen. Henry N .... I, 1 N. Y. H. A.
Bates, O. N .... Signal Corps, U. S. A.
Bunker, Charles C .... A, 1 N. Y. Mtd. Rifles
Buxton, Richard F .... 2 Batt. Mass. L. A.
Brosmer, Frank W .... K, 2 N. Y. V.
Bixby, E. G .... G, 5 N. Y. H. A.
Burrows, L. G .... A, 144 N. Y.
Bunn, C. E .... H, 152 N. Y.
Blanchard, A. S .... A, 1 Ind. H. A.
Benton, O. A .... D, 146 N. Y.

Butts, E L .... A, 1 L. A.
Barnes, A. M .... H, 152 N. Y.
Beeman, W. B .... H, 152 N. Y.
Brown, S. H .... C, 134 N. Y.
Bradley Wilbur .... D, 144 N. Y.
Barnes, D. C .... G, 3 N. Y C.
Bonen, Zebulon .... 121 N. Y.
Butts, J. P .... I, 144 N. Y.
Barto, E .... Rec. Unknown
Barnes, Dennis R ....
Breuer, E. W .... G, 3 N. Y. C.
Bronson, W. E .... D, 144 N. Y.
Buckley, G D .... 8 Batt, L. A
Carl, Thomas .... A, 177 N. Y.
Case, Dr. Meigs .... 43 N. Y.
Colvin, Geo. N .... H, 2 Penn.
Crockett, J. H .... H, 16 H. A.
Chandler, Marvin .... G, 144 N. Y.
Cleveland, J. B .... B, 41 N. Y.
Cassady, James .... A, 43 N. Y.
Dimmock, A. D .... G, 187 Penn.
Driggs, Edgar S .... A, 1 N. Y. Eng.
Davis, E. H ....
Elliott, J .... I, 144 N. Y.
Ellis, John .... M, 6 H. A.
Ford, C. E .... (Elsworth) C, 44 N. Y.
Fletcher, J. B .... A, 95 Ills
Fox, R. L .... A, 1 N. Y.
Ferguson, Lyman .... M, 3 N. Y.
Howland, J. W .... K, 47 N. Y.
Houghtaling, A E .... F, 96 N. Y.
Hall, Edgar .... B, 144 N. Y.
Holdridge, Russell .... G, 1 N. Y. Eng.
Hollister, L .... I, 121 N. Y.
Harmon, Orlon .... C, 27 N. Y.

Harris, Floyd...	K, 185 N. Y.
Hemstreet, N L.	K, 76 N. Y.
Huggins, S.	K, 93 N. Y.
Ingalls, John C.	G, 3 N. Y. C.
Jackson, L. M. S.	D, 144 N. Y.
Jaynes, E. O.	G, 176 N. Y.
Jewell, N. D.	D, 3 N. Y. C.
Kenyon, James	C, 43 N. Y.
Lee, H. N.	C, 80 N. Y.
Low, Charles E.	G, 14 N. Y.
Marks, Henry	I, 1 Md. V.
Mackley, George A.	I, 144 N. Y.
Morris, William H.	G, 1 Eng.
Marx, H.	Steamer Montgomery
Murdock, Emory	G, 6 N. Y. C.
Munson, M. D.	D, 144 N. Y.
Morgan, E. J., M. D.	B. 15 N. Y. H. A.
Miller, Adelmer	I, 144 N. Y.
Mosher, J. H.	U. S. Marine Corps
Maxwell, G. F.	8 Ind Batt.
Moreness, H. W.	C, 1 Eng.
Olin, William	I, 121 N. Y.
Owens, C. R.	H, 6 N. Y. A.
Olin, S. M.	K, 121 N. Y.
Peck, William H.	G, 8 N. Y. C.
Paul, W. B. S.	I, 91 N. Y.
Pogue, John	144 N. Y.
Potter, C. A.	E. 10 N. Y. H. A.
Reynolds, E. A.	G, 8 N. Y. C.
Roe, Joshua	I, 1 N. Y. Eng.
Rollins, Charles	K, 144 N. Y.
Roberts, James	G, 3 N. Y. C.
Rowe, Adelbert	K, 144 N. Y.
Rowe, James	I, 144 N Y.
Rathbun, Corbin	I 144 N. Y.

Richardson, Egbert..L, 22 N. Y. C
Reynolds, George W. (Capt.)...........................K, 144 N. Y.
Reynolds, George..G, 3 N. Y. C
Southard, John W..8 N. Y. Ind Batt.
Safford, M. A...F, 22 N. Y. C.
Swart, Elias B..C, 144 N. Y.
Seegar, C. F..A, 43 N. Y.
Southworth, W. A..A, 89 N. Y.
Vanauken, J. W...F, 137 N. Y.
Whitman, H. C..G, 3 N Y.C.
Weidman, Peter...H, 144 N Y.
Winn, Charles...6, 15 N. Y. H. A.
Wager F. F..H, 156 N. Y.
Whitmarsh, H...
Walling, Abner A..I, 144 N. Y.
Wilbur, C L...I, 144 N. Y.
Westcott, C. J...I, 121 N. Y.

Graves Decorated by E. D. Farmer Post.

WAR OF 1861—1865.

Alger, David	Grant, W. F.	Rowe, George.
Burton, Warren.	Green, Erastus.	Sabin, Algernon
Benedict, Joseph,	Hudson, W. H.	Strait, Jacob
Beach, Robert	Keenan, Malcom	Schemerhorn, P.
Butts, C. H.	Lansing, David	Snow, Willis W.
Baxter, I. E.	Mereness, Wm.	Strait, Harrison
Babcock, S A.	Miller, John	Thompson, Charles
Brightman, E.	Mallary, G. S.	Van Alstine, H. B.

Butts, Lewis   Maynard, T. F.   Van Lovan, Jonas
Brownell, John   Mickle, William   Winn, John W.
Brewer, Charles   Marble, E. S   Wolf, Ira D
Cutshaw, Elvin   Marble, James   Winne, Alexander
Cutshaw, Warren   Moak, J. I.   Watkins, C. A.
Driggs, John   Potter, Ezra G.   Wiles, Peter C
Fuller, Wm. D.   Pratt, Leonard   Whitney, Joseph
Fish, Phineas C.   Perine, P. S.   Watkins, Alonzo R.
Goodsell, F. J.   Pardoe, J. F., Jr.   Weidman, Frank
Greene Lewis   Packard E.   Wickham, Henry
Graves, Nathan   Packard, A F.   Watkins Albert

OTHER WARS.

Thos. Mearness, Revolution,   Peter Brewer, Revolution.
Jeremy Meareness, 1812,   Captain Samuel Bixby, 1812,
James Pendleton, 1812,   Barth. McGuire, 1812,
Frederick Bornt. 1812,   Stephen Barnes. 1882.

C. C. Siver Post, No. 124,

UNADILLA, N. Y.

Regular Meetings every Saturday Evening at G. A. R Hall.

THIS POST was organized Sept. 13, 1879; charter received and mustered into the Department of New York, October 4, 1879, by Mustering Officer L. Coe Young, of Watrous Post, No. 30, of Binghamton, N. Y.

The Post was named in honor of C. C. Siver, a respected citizen and a distinguished soldier of the village of Unadilla. He was born in the town of Meridith, Delaware county. While quite young he went with his father's family to the town of Sidney, passing his early boyhood days upon his father's farm, and in going to school. He, about the year 1868, took up his residence in the city of New York, from which place he enlisted upon the breaking out of the Rebellion, in the 8th N. Y. N. G—three months men—and was in the first battle of Bull Run. At the expiration of his term of service he returned to Sidney, soon after going South again as sutler's agent; was taken sick with typhoid fever in a few months and was soon brought home, where he remained until the 144th regiment, N. Y. S. V., was organized, when he again sought the battlefield, and joining that famous regiment, was mustered in at Elmira, N. Y., Sept. 27, 1862, receiving a commission as First Lieutenant of Co. D, Oct. 4, 1862. Was detailed as aid to General ———, and acting assistant adjutant of the post stationed at Hilton Head, S. C., on the staff of Brig. General E. E. Potter, and promoted to Captain April 18, 1864. Was mustered out of the service June 25, 1865, returning to Sidney. Soon after married and removed to Unadilla, and in company with T. G. North, bought the interest of Samuel North in the hardware trade. But a short time after this Samuel North and David Siver, with their sons, T. G. North and C. C. Siver, established the banking house of North, Siver & Co. In 1870, his health failing, he disposed of his property and business interests in Unadilla, and went west in company with his friend, Asa G. Strong, now residing in Oneouta, in the hopes of regaining his health, but it was too late, the fatal desease was deeply seated, and in July, 1872, he returned to Unadilla, and died, Nov. 21, 1872. He was buried the Sunday following, with Masonic honors, eighty Sir Knights of the Norwich Commandry, and the F. and A. M. of the Unadilla, Walton, Delhi and Franklin Lodges, the 103d regiment band from Norwich, and a large procession of relatives and friends following the remains to the cemetery. The services at the grave, under the auspices of the Knights Templar, was of an imposing character. He was a model soldier, a true friend and neighbor, and a respected citizen, faithful to every trust. That the members of the Post cherish and honor his memory, is demonstrated by the many floral tributes placed upon his grave with each recurring Memorial day.

Frank G. Bolls was born at Oxford, N. Y., in 1833, and educated at the Oxford Academy: completing his education he engaged in the hardware business at Unadilla. N. Y. When the first call for three months' men was made he left his business in charge of his brother and enlisted in Co. F, 121st N. Y. V., and was mustered into service at Mohawk, N. Y., as Second Lieutenant, he having recruited a number of men for Co. F. By reason of poor health, caused by a fall near White Oak Church, while out on picket duty, and a sprained back, he resigned in February, 1863, and returned to Unadilla to his former business. He was a charter member of Siver Post, and was elected first Commander in August, 1879, serving until Jan. 1, 1880. He was Post Master at Unadilla during Cleveland's administration.

Warren Curtis, Commander elected to succeed Mr. Bolles, was born at Franklin, Delaware county, N. Y., Oct. 24, 1850. When three years old removed to Unadilla, N. Y., and while attending school at that place, enlisted at Norwich, N. Y., in August, 1863 (when only twelve years old) as a private in Co. E, the famous Irish regiment, 69th N. Y. Vols., and was mustered into the U. S. service under Captain Peter Sweeney, Aug. 27, 1863. Ordered to the front, going to Petersburg, Va. Soon after enlisting was made sergeant, and appointed drummer in Co. E, 69th, N. Y. V. His record is that of his regiment, participating in all its battles until the close of the war. The record of that famous regiment stands without a peer; composed entirely of the patriotic sons of the sturdy Celtic race. The heroic deeds of the 69th N. Y. Vols. on the battle field can never be effaced as long as time shall last. And when the memories of war are growing dim, the gratitude of the loyal American citizen of the Anglo-Saxon race will be just as keen and appreciative as in the darkest hour of danger, to the noble men of Irish birth, who did such splendid service that the country to which they had sworn allegiance and loved so well might live. Curtis was discharged and mustered out of the service at Alexandria, June 5th, 1865, returning to Sidney in poor health, where he remained an invalid for eighteen months. In 1867 he went to Binghamton, N. Y., and entered the Commercial College, where he completed his education. Afterwards he accepted a position in the engineer corps of the Midland (now the P. O. & W.) R. R. In 1871 he went to Franklin, Delaware county, and worked at and learned the tin-smith trade. In 1874 went to Illinois, where he worked at his trade until the winter of the same year, when he returned to Unadilla, where he has since resided, and at the present time has charge of the the tin shop connected with the hardware house of W. H. Crocker. He was a charter member of C. C. Sivier Post, and at its organization in October, 1876, was elected Junior Vice Commander, and in the December following was elected Commander to serve during the year 1880. He being but 29 years old when elected, is entitled to the distinction and the honor of being the youngest Past Commander in the State. His administration was one of thorough discipline, the Post becoming one of influence and prominence in the department. He was again elected Commander in 1889, and served with distinction, winning renewed honor as a presiding officer. He is now serving his third term as adjutant of the Post. He was Mustering Officer at the organization of the Charles Bradford Post, of Sidney Plains; also in company with Coe F. Young, Mustering Officer at the organization of C. A. Shepherd Post, 189, of Otego, and was on the staff of Coe F. Young during his term as department Commander. He is at the present time foreman of S. S. North Hose Co., a prominent Mason, and at present Junior Warden of Freedom Lodge, of Unadilla, N. Y., and has held the civil office of collector of the town of Unadilla. Servimg during his term of office in the different societies which have elected him, he has honored himself as well as the society which he has represented.

A. J. Thorn, Commander for the year 1881, was born in

the town of Maryland in October, 1839, receiving a common school education. He enlisted in September, 1864, as a private in Co. G, 6th N. Y. C. No more faithful or better soldier entered the service. He was always happy and was poor society for those troubled with the blues. He served with his regiment, participating in all skirmishes and battles until discharged in June, 1865, when he returned to Portlandville. He contracted a severe cold in March, 1865, while going from Shanandoah to Petersburg, from which he never recovered, and died at Unadilla, Dec. 13, 1889, leaving an estimable wife, now residing at Unadilla, and an active member of the W. R. C., to mourn his loss. He was buried at Portlandville, N. Y., his funeral being largely attended by friends and comrades of the G. A. R. from Otsego county. The Sons of Veterans Camp at Unadilla was named in his honor.

Francis D. Butler was born May 29th, 1833, at Unadilla, N. Y., receiving a common school education; at the age of 17 left school to learn the carpenter and joiner trade. On the first day of September, 1862, he enlisted as private in Co. G, 152 N. Y., under Capt. E. C. Gilbert, and was mustered into the U. S. service at Mohawk, Oct. 15, 1862. Was ordered to Chain Bridge, defense of Washington, and in February, 1863, to Washington for guard duty; in April to Suffork, Va.; in June to Yorktown and up the Peninsula under Keys, through the Peninsula campaign of 1883, participating in the battle of the Wilderness, and afterwards ordered to re-enforce Mead at the battle of Gettysburgh. June 24, 1863, by reason of the riot, ordered to New York city; in October, 1863, joined the Army of the Potomac under Hancock in the Second Corps. Was with the 152d up to and including the capture of Lee; was wounded in front of Petersburg. Was made corporal in the fall of 1862, and in February, 1863, was promoted to First Sergeant, October. 1864, to First Lieutenant, and Dec. 26. 1864, promoted to Captain. Mustered out at Washington in July, 1865. Returned to Unadilla and to his former trade as carpenter and joiner. Was a charter member of his post, and elected as Commander to serve during the year 1882. His administration was such as to receive the approbation of the members of the post, and he was again elected to serve during the year 1883. Record same as regiment.

David R. Harris was born Aug. 9, 1839, at Columbus. Chenango county, N. Y. When six years old he went to Palmyra, Mich., where he attended the district schools; in 1848 returned to Lawrence, Otsego county, N. Y., removing in 1850 to Otego, and in 1852 to Edemston, going from there to Brookfield. returning in 1854 to Edemston, where he completed his education. Enlisted Aug. 5, 1862, as a private in Co. F., 121 N. Y. Vols., and mustered into the U. S. service. Aug. 23d, as corporal and ordered to Washington at once. Was under fire at Crampton Pass, South Mountain; thence to Antietam, and after battle to Bakersville. Was with the Army of the Potomac until June 21, 1864, participating with his regiment in the battles of Gettysburg, Rappahannock Station. Miles Run, Wilderness, Spotsylvania, Cold Harbor and Petersburg. Was wounded at the battle of Petersburg, June 21, 1864, sent to the field hospital and thence to Carver hospital, Washington, where he remained from July 4 to July 12, 1864, when he was transferred to Mount Pleasant, remaining there until May 17, 1865, when he was by reason of general orders discharged. Returned to New Berlin, and in 1870 took up his residence in Unadilla, where he has since resided. Was a charter member and one of those who procured names for the organization of C. C. Sivier post, and elected Chaplain at the first meeting and re-elected until 1884; was elected Commander two years, 1885-86; was on the Department Staff as aid to Commander Clarkson. Always at his post, his administration was such as to strengthen the enviable reputation the post had already atrained under the wise management of his immediate predecessors.

L. J. Post, charter member and Past Commander of the post, elected in December, 1877, to serve during the following year, was born in Unadilla, attending the district school at that place, and completing his education at the Unadilla academy. He was by occupation a farmer, and left the farm to fight for the flag he loved so well, and in just five days after he had enrolled his name he was facing the enemy. Enlisted at Deposit, N. Y., Oct. 17, 1861; mustered into the United States service at Elmira, N. Y., October 19th, and joining his company, which was already in the field, at Fairfax Seminary, Oct. 22, 1861. Participated in the following battles, with his company: West Point, Mechanicsville, Gaines Mills, including the seven days fighting on the Peninsula, at Crampton Pass, Anteitam, Fredericksburg and Second Rull Run. He was discharged May 31, 1863. Re-enlisting on the 4th day of January, 1864, as private in Co. A, 13th Heavy Artillery, and mustered in at Fort Schuyler, Feb. 1, 1864, joining his company about Feb. 8, at Griswold, near Portsmouth, Va; May 4, 1864, was in the charge at Bermuda Hundred and at Petersburg June 23 to July 30, 1864. His battery was engaged, doing splendid service at different times, at Dutch Gap and Bermuda front. The battery was consolidated with and discharged as Co. H, 6th N. Y. Heavy Artillery. As presiding officer of the Post he displayed more than ordinary executive ability, and his administration was such as to merit the approbation of the comrades of the Post, and retain its standing and high rank which this Post had already attained in the Department.

Robert S. Balestier, Commander for 1890-91, was born at Chicago, Ill., Oct. 20, 1838; in 1848 went with his parents to New York, where he attended school, and graduated at Union College in 1857. Two years later, in 1859, he made a voyage around the world, going to San Francisco and China, and back to New York, arriving at that place in February, 1861, and April 14, 1861, enlisted in Co. K, 79th N. Y. Vols.; was commissioned Second Lieutenant and mustered into the United States service May 20th, 1861, under Captain Shillinglow; resigned July 3d, 1861, and re-enlisted and was commissioned Second Lieutenant in the 3d New York Independent Battery in September, 1861. Resigned again in February, 1862, enlisting in the Marine Corps, in March, 1862; and was discharged by special order at Cairo, Ill., Oct. 14, 1863, and received a commission in the United States navy, Oct. 20, 1863. Served in the Mississippi squadron on board the Linden throughout the siege of Vicksburg under Foot, and with Banks' expedition. Remained in the Mississippi squadron until June 3, 1865, when he was discharged and mustered out at New York. Received a sabre wound at Yorktown in 1862. After leaving the service he accepted a position as clerk, and has been in the express and railroad business for 23 years. Has resided in Unadilla since 1866, and is a charter member of C. C. Siver Post; was officer of the day during the year 1875; his administration as Commander during his first term, 1890, was noted for promptness in its dealing with the Department, and he was again elected for the second time, to serve during 1891. When he surrendered to Mr. R. G. Brown, his successor as Commander, the affairs of C. C. Siver Post, No. 124, were second to none as to rank and sociability. He served one year as aide-de camp on the Department Staff, and on the National Staff during the year 1889, as aide-de-camp, attached to General Alger's Staff.

The present Commander, Robert G. Brown, was born at Albany, N. Y. in 1844; attended school in that city until fifteen years old; found employment in a hat factory. July 13, 1862, he enlisted as a private in Co. E, 113th N. Y. Vols., and Aug. 18, 1862, was ordered to Fort Reno, and the defense of Washington. This regiment was changed to the artillery service and known as the 7th N. Y. Heavy Artillery. Battery E was detatched and ordered to garrison Batteries Cameron and Scott on the Potomac, near Chain Bridge; Sept. 3, ordered to garrison Fort Gaines; Nov. 12, joined the regiment at Fort Reno for winter quarters; in the spring of 1863 reported to Battery Smead, and in May, 1864, ordered to Bell Plains Landing on the Potomac; to Fredericksburg; thence to Spotsylvania Court House, where they engaged in a brisk fight, the rebels attempting to capture their wagon train; they drove the rebels from Spotsylvania to Tolopotomy Creek, out of their breastworks, capturing their front lines, and holding their position; going from there to North Anna, making a splendid charge, routing the enemy and capturing many guns, amunition, etc; thence to Cold Harbor and on to Petersburg; June 16, 1864, made a dashing charge on the rebel fort, and amid the cheering of the men, were about to gain a victory, when the rebels in large force made a successful flank movement to the right of the battery, capturing Captain Norman H. Moors, and about one-third of his command; the balance of the battery, under Lieutenant E. H. Wilsey, were brought safely to the Union lines, remaining some time doing picket duty; ordered down on the left of the line, and in battle at Ream's Station; Brown was wounded in the thigh, but did not leave his regiment. Feb. 22, 1865, the regiment was ordered to Baltimore for guard duty at Fort McHenry, and discharged June 16, 1865. He returned to Albany and learned the stone cutting trade; in 1867 he went to Unadilla, and in 1871 embarked in the marble and tombstone business; in 1888 he went on a farm. Joined C. C. Sivier Post in 1879; was Senior Vice during the year 1881, and Quartermaster for several years. He is a respected citizen and comrade and an afable gentleman. As presiding officer of the Post he has proved to be the right man in the right place.

Francis W. Sisson was born at Unadilla, July 26, 1842, attending the common school until 1859, then going to Gilbertsville Academy for two years, completing his education at the Delaware Institute, at Franklin, N. Y. Sept. 6, 1862, he enlisted, in the town of Butternuts, as a private in Co. G, 152d N. Y. V., going to the defence of Washington at Chain Bridge, and in February, 1863, to Washington for guard duty; while here sent to Douglass Hospital, and soon afterward transferred to Chestnut Street Hospital, from which he was discharged and joined his regiment at New York, where they had been ordered in June, 1863, during the riot in that city. The regiment was ordered to the front in October, 1863, joining the 1st brigade, 2d division, Hancock's Corps, Army of the Potomac. Participated in the battles of Miles Run, Wilderness, Spotsylvania, Cold Harbor, Petersburg and Deep Bottom; was detailed in May, as orderly on Gen. Owens' staff, but owing to the arrest of Gen. Owens, after the battle of Cold Harbor, by order of Gen. Gibbons, was ordered to his regiment; engaged in battle before Petersburg, and was wounded at Ream's Station, Aug. 25, 1864, was picked up by an officer of the 9th corps, who procured an ambulance and had him taken to the camp hospital, Petersburg, refreshed by a cup of coffee, and conveyed to Emery Hospital, Washington; he remained here during the winter of 1864-5; procured at thirty days' furlough and came North. His wound breaking out again he returned to the hospital and remained until May, 1865, when he rejoined his regiment at Munson Hill, Alexandria; was promoted to corporal and detailed as clerk in the adjutant's office. Was mustered out of service at Munson Hill, July 30, 1865. He returned to Unadilla, and in 1870 went into the mercantile business at Wells Bridge; was Postmaster during Cleveland's administration. Disposing of his business in 1890, to his son, he returned to Unadilla, and in company with Fred. L. Joyce, embarked in the furniture business. Joined the C. C. Siver Post, but while residing at Wells Bridge took a discharge; returning to Unadilla, he rejoined the Post, and is at this time its efficient Quartermaster. He resides with his family, consisting of wife, and daughter, ten years old, two sons, W. H. and B. F., residing at Wells Bridge, N. Y.

Horace Edgar Bailey, was born at Masonville, N. Y., Aug. 5, 1840; attended the common schools, completing his education, in 1860, at the Delaware Literary institute, Franklin, N. Y.; taught school for three winters at Masonville and Oneonta. He enlisted on the 25th of August, 1862, in Co. B, 144th N. Y. V., and was mustered into the United States service at Elmira, N. Y., on the 22d day of Sept. 1862, going to Camp Bliss, Upton Hill Va.; to Cloud Mills, in the defence of the Capitol. In the spring of 1863 was ordered to Fairfax Seminary; thence to Suffolk, Va., durtng Longstreet's seige, from April 12 to May 14; participated, June 8th, at Yorktown, Va., in Gen. Key's demonstration against Richmond. Joined the Army of the Potomac, 10th Corps, in July, 1863, at Berlin, Md., and July 19th crossed the river on pontoon bridge, following Lee through Virginia toward Richmond. Aug. 6th the regiment was assigned to the Department of the South, and embarked on transports for Folly Island, and on the 12th sent to Morris Island, doing duty there during Gen. Gilmore's operations at the bombardment of Sumter at the seige of Charleston, in August and September, 1863. Soon after retiring to Folly Island, did picket duty, and engaged in several demonstrations against the enemy; near Folly Island, Bailey commanded the company in the first field fight in which this regiment had engaged. Feb. 15, 1864, sent to Florida, raiding, etc.; in June returned to Hilton Head, the headquarters of the regiment. During the latter part of 1864, the regiment accompanied Gen. Dick Foster in his co-operative movements with Sherman at Honey Hill, Nov. 30, and Devaux Neck, Dec. 6 and 8; Coosawhatchie, Dec. 9, 1864; also at James Island during Thomas's triumphant march through South Carolina; at Bulls Bay and up the banks of the Santee river, and along the coast under the command of the gallant Gen. Porter, doing excellent service for the cause in which they were engaged. Bailey was wounded three times at Honey Hill. He enlisted as a private, was soon after promoted to Second Sergeant, and later to Orderly Sergeant; for distinguished services in the field was promoted to Second Lieutenant and discharged as First Lieutenant in command of the company. He is now residing at Unadilla with his family—an estimable wife, a son 21 years old, and a daughter, age 19. He is Past High Priest of Unadilla Chapter, trustee of the Unadilla Academy, an honored and respected citizen and neighbor.

POST OFFICERS.

R G. Brown..........................Commander.
Benjamin Nichols...................Senior Vice Commander.
O. W. Briggs......................Junior Vice Commander.
Warren Curtis.....................Adjutant.
Frank M. Sisson...................Quartermaster.
D. R. Harris......................Chaplain.
D. C. Potter......................Surgeon.
P. P. Shaw........................Officer of the Day.
W. W. Carver......................Officer of the Guard.

Past Commanders.

F. G. Bolles,   Warren Curtts,   A. J. Thorn,
D. R. Harris,   L. J. Post,   F. D. Butler.
A. H. C. Brown,   S. Northrup,   R. S. Balestier.

List of Members.

Briggs, J. W..E, 2 N. Y. A.
Bartlett, Homer C...G, 1 N. Y. Eng.
Bolles, F. G..F, 121 N. Y.
Balestier, R. S...B, 79 N. Y.
Brown, Robert G..............113 N. Y. V.,; E, 7 N. Y. H. A.
Butler, F. D., Capt.......................................G, 152 N. Y.
Bailey, H. E..H, 144 N. Y.
Bell, Chauncey..F, 121 N. Y.
Bogart, James P...I, 127 N. Y.
Blanchard, William..B, 90 N. Y.
Crocker, H. B...K, 89 N. Y.
Curtis, Warren..E, 69 N. Y.
Carley, Jefferson...A, 1 N. Y. Eng.
Cornell, Cornelius..K, Mich. Res.
Curtis, Charles...F, 15 Ill. Art
Cleaver, Warren W...B, 144 N. Y.
Cuyler, William D...H, 144 N. Y.
Fisk, George..K, 10 N. Y. C.

Greene I. R... ....E, 2 N. Y. Art.
Gilbert, John B..E, 2 N. Y. Art.
Harris, D. R...................................... ....F, 121 N. Y.
Hyatt, C. S................ ....I, 117 N. Y.
Hotaling, William G.....................................A, 7 N. Y. Art.
Harris. J. S...B, 102 N. Y.
Jones Samuel.............................. ....D, 22 Cal. Cav.
Lawrence, A. J............. ....B, 56 N. Y.
Leach, Horace Y...B, 114 N. Y.
Mott, Leroy..K, 89 N. Y.
Mudford, William.. ....L, 22 N Y.
Mackley, Morgan...I 144 N. Y.
Northrup, Samuel...L, 22 N. Y. C.
Nichols, Benjamin..L, 20 N. Y. C.
Nichols, David..E, 2 N. Y. Art.
Olmstead, Kellog.............. ....B, 144 N. Y.
Olds, Alonzo..F, 121 N. Y.
Olds, Jabez..............................C, 144 N. Y.; 1 N. Y. Eng.
Post, L. J............... ....C, 27, N. Y.
Page, Joseph...................................13 N. Y. Art.
Phillips, Sylvester....... ....I, 1 U. S. Cav.
Kifenbark, T E...C, 114 N. Y.
Rifenberg, William............ ....
Redfield, Elisha..F, 144 N. Y.
Sweet, J. J. .... Surgeon.
Sisson, Frank M..G, 152 N. Y.
Snyder, E. E...G, 121 N. Y. Art.
Slade, Charles L............ ....E, 2 N. Y. H. A.
Stoddard, C... ....B, 144 N. Y.
Slade, Richard...E, 2 N. Y. H. A.
Shaw P. P..F, 27 N. Y.
Ten broeck, Jerry......... ....F, 2 N. Y. C.
Vincent, George A...........................F, 34 Mass. Vol
Vanderwort, John............... ......C, 27 N. Y.; 1 N. Y. Eng.
Warner Sylvanus C..K, 144 N. Y.

CARR & CO.,
DEALERS IN
Fresh & Salt Meats,
Fish, Oysters, Poultry, Game, Etc.

Pure Home-made Lard.

☞ Cash Paid for HIDES, PELTS FURS and SKINS.

166 MAIN STREET, UNADILLA, N. Y.

PHOTOGRAPHIC ✠ STUDIO,

A. Wheeler.

Pictures enlarged to any size.

Finest work, and guaranteed.

ALL SIZES TAKEN FROM LIFE.

Depot Street, Unadilla, N. Y.

Unadilla Steam Laundry,

L. O. FROST, PROPRIETOR.
11 DEPOT STREET, UNADILLA, N. Y.

The best equipped Laundry between Albany and Binghamton. Latest Improved Machinery for doing

FIRST CLASS WORK,

Lace curtains and **draperies made** to look like new.

Laundry called for and delivered in the village.

IN MEMORIAM.

Mulford, John L.................................L, 101 N. Y.
Place, William..................................H, 89 N. Y.
Thorn, A. J....................................G, 6 N. Y. C.
Thornton John..................................C, 147 N. Y.

A. J. THORN CAMP, S. OF V., 119.
Unadilla, N. Y.

Meets Friday Evenings at G. A. R. Hall.

This Camp was organized April 25, 1890, and mustered by F. M. H. Butts, of Oneonta, N. Y., with the following charter members: W. H. Crooker, Frank F. Butler, Charles E. Clever, Charles W. Jones, W. J. Palmer, Eugene A. Houck, R. J. Vandervoort, Tolo C. Graves, John H. Milliken, John S. Nichols, Louis Hemier.

On electing officers of the Camp, although having plenty of material from which to choose a Commander, the members made a most excellent choice in the person of W. H. Crooker, one of the most prominent young business men of Unadilla. Born at Unadilla, N. Y., in May,

The Bargain Bazaar.

Tobacco, Segars, House Furnishing Goods, China and Glassware, Dolls, Games and Toys, Suspenders and Neckwear, Teas, Coffees and Spices, Canned Goods, Crackers, &c.

⁕ General News Office, ⁕

All the latest novels on hand, and orders taken for periodicals and magazines.

THE CHOICEST CONFECTIONS,
NOTIONS AND NOVELTIES. STATIONERY AND SCHOOL SUPPLIES.

JOHN N. HANFORD,
278 MAIN STREET, (Whitney Block), UNADILLA, N. Y.

Otego ⁕ Valley ⁕ Hotel,
[Formerly Brownell's Hotel.]

Hartwick, N. Y.

This well-known Hotel has been thoroughly renovated and every improvement made that could add to the comfort of guests.

GOOD SAMPLE ROOM FOR COMMERCIAL TRAVELERS

Rates, $1.50 per day.   H. W. WOOD, Mgr.

1851, and educated at the Academy at that place; leaving school in 1870; learned the tinsmith trade at Oneonta, N. Y., and in 1871 entered the employ of North & Siver, at Unadilla. In 1873 accepted a position with J. H. Lathrop, at Norwich, N. Y.; went to Bainbridge in 1874 in the employ of Isaac Sterling, remaining until 1880; then going to Masonville, Delaware county, he embarked in the general hardware trade, where he did a successful business and made many friends; disposing of his business interests at that place in 1890, he returned to Unadilla and accepted a position as traveling salesman in the employ of Babcock & Stowell of Binghamton, N. Y., remaining in their employ but a short time however, when he purchased the stock of Cone & Bolles, hardware dealers at Unadilla, and the following spring sold his stock to C. H. Stebbins, and in the fall of 1891 succeeded W. H. Heslop, general hardware dealer, corner of Main and Clifton streets, Unadilla, where he is now doing a thriving business. The administration of his office has been attended with the same business tact as is given to his private business. The Camp has wisely retained him to succeed himself as his terms of office have expired, the roster of the Camp showing about thirty members and is steadily increasing. He is a most companionable officer and gentleman, and through his influence the Camp is fast becoming renowned for great zeal and sociability.

Camp Officers.

W. H. Crooker......................Captain.
Charles Tenbroeck................First Sergeant
Lewis Heimer......................First Lieutenant,
John H. Milliken,.................Second Lieutenant.
C. W. Jones.......................Chaplain.
W. J. Palmer......................Quartermaster Sergant.
John S Nichols........... ....Sergeant of the Guard.

Isaac Olds..........................Corporal.
Burt Palmer........................Camp Guard.
Wolcott Balistier...................Principal Musician.

LIST OF MEMBERS.

Butler, F. E.	Johnson, Leonard	Palmer, W. J.
Balistier, Bob., Jr.	Jordan, W. E.	Palmer, Fred. D.
Crooker, W. H.	Lang, A. M.	Palmer, Albert
Cleaves, Charles	Milliken, John	Ripley Benjamin
Elwell, Burt E.	Nichols, John H.	Tenbrock, C. C.
Graves, T. C.	Olmstead, John	Tenbrock, Jerry
Heimer, Louis	Olds, William G.	Vandervoort, J. H.
Houck, O. E.	Olds, John H.	Vandervoort, R. J.
Jones, Charles W.	Olds, Isaac	

H. N. Duro Post, No. 653,

HARTWICK, N. Y.

Regular Meetings first and third Saturday Evenings of each Month, at the Marsh House.

THIS POST was organized through the personal efforts of L. W. Murdock; its charter was received Nov. 4, 1891, and mustered into the department of New York, Nov. 14, 1891, by Comrade John N. Vosburg, of Hall Post, Laurens, N. Y., as mustering officer.

The Post was named in honor of Horatio N. Duro, a brave soldier, who was killed while charging the rebel pickets in front of Fort Fisher, March 26, 1864. He was shot through the head and fell by the side of Lester W. Murdock. The same night his remains were brought int the Union lines and sent to New Lisbon, Otsego county, N. Y., where he was buried, his funeral being largely attended by friends and relatives.

At the first meeting of the Post Lester W. Murdock was elected Commander. He was born at Hartwick, N. Y., February, 18, 1837, where he was educated, and enlisted Aug. 1, 1862, as a private in Co. E, 121st Regiment, N. Y. V. Was at Crampton Pass, Sept. 14, 1862, was struck by a fragment of shell, which sent him tumbling down a steep bank. Sergeant Hawley, of his company, ordered him to go to a barn, about a mile away, for medical assistance; remained there about six days without any attention, when a stranger, a Mr. Little, informed him that there were several sick and wounded soldiers at Jefferson, seven miles from the barn, and kindly offered to let him ride in his cart, if he wished to go. They had gone about two miles when the conversation turned upon the cause of the war; his new made friend suddenly brought his horse to a halt, and ordered Murdock to get out, as he would not allow a black Abolitionist to ride in his cart. Although very lame and sore he managed to travel the other five milles in as many hours; arrived at Jefferson and was cared for by citizens for four weeks. Among the new acquaintances made there were Dr. Culver. Dr. Crum, George Hoffman and Thomas M. Culler. May 3, 1863, was again wounded by a spent ball passing through his clothes, cutting his suspenders and shirt, raising a contusion five inches long and as large as a broomstick. It the fall of 1863, at Rappahannock Station, he responded to a call for a volunteer to guard the bridge which spanned the river at that place. At 2 o'clock the next morning a rebel was seen to approach at the farther end and set it on fire; he fired at him and received two shots in return. At the battle of the Wilderness, May 6, 1864, was taken prisoner; in an effort to escape he was shot in the neck by an officer, with a revolver; on the 10th of the same month he took his place in the ranks, and participated in the memorable bayonet charge at Spotsylvania. He remained with his regiment to Gettysburg, and through the campaign near Charlestown, Va.; August 21, 1864, while skirmishing, was struck in the right side by a spent ball, fracturing his sixth and seventh ribs: October 19, in the battle at Cedar Creek, while assisting Lieutenant Johnson, who had been wounded, to his feet, a ball passed through his coffee-pot, strapped to his knapsack: near Petersburg the regiment was exposed to an annoying fire, which had killed one man and wounded several others; he was sent to ascertain from whence came the firing; after penetrating the dense forest for half a mile he saw a man from the 2d Corps, who said he was sent to see, if possible, why their supposed enemy did not return the fire. March 25, 1865, was again wounded in the left leg in front of Fort Fisher. Discharged at Albany, June 25, 1865, and returned to Hartwick. He organized Duro Post and was chosen its first Commander, and in December, 1891, again elected Commander to serve during 1892. His administration has been such as to place the Post in the front rank for sociability and promptness, in the Department. He is an honored and respected citizen, who is always ready with his time and means to advance the interests of the G. A. R. The building occupied by the Post, which was kindly placed at their disposal during the existence of their charter by Mr. H. K. Marsh, has been put in order and made most inviting by Comrade Murdock. He is now residing at Hartwick with his family, an estimable wife, and two daughters, ages 11 and 13.

William Blanchard, charter member of Post, was born in Franklin, Delaware county, in 1833; educated at the common schools; enlisted in June, 1862, and mustered in at Norwich, Sept. 21, 1862, as private in Co. K, 114th N. Y. Vols.; went by canal to Binghamton, and thence to Elmira and to Baltimore, where he was one of ten selected from each companay to do police duty; remained there until after charter election; Dec. 13. 1862, went aboard steamer Thames, under General Banks, for Fortress Monroe; thence to Cape Henry and from Cape Henry, with fifteen vessels, for Cape Hatteras, experiencing a rough voyage; ran up a signal of distress and was towed into Hilton Head by the Erricson. The storm was so severe that the life boats were of no avail; the two boats were tied together; the water being three feet in the boat, and with no food or water to drink they lay in the water for 36 hours; remained at Hilton Head 12 days, and went aboard another boat, Jan. 9th, to Carlton; contracted fever, went to New Orleans, and was sent to regimental hospital; thence to Brazo City, May 8, 1863; was in skirmish at Irish Bend, May 10, 1863. He had a relapse, and was sent back to New Orleans, and discharged from the service in July, 1863. Returned to Hartwick, where he is now residing with his wife and daughter, aged 21; He is at the present time Senior Vice Commander of the Post.

Emmet M. Irons, a brave soldier, enlisting in Co. E, 121st N. Y. Vols.; always on duty and engaging in the battles of this famous regiment; wounded at Salem Heights May 3, 1863, in left temple by musket ball; April 2, 1865, in front of Petersburg, struck by a spent ball between the shoulders, and wounded in the face and neck by the concussion of a shell, April 6, 1865, but remained with regiment, fighting to the last. He is at the present time Officer of the Day of Duro Post.

William Holdridge was born in Monroe county, in 1849; enlisted August 25, 1864, in Co. B, 9th Heavy Artillery; was wounded in front of Fort Fisher, near Petersburg, March 25, 1865, by a gun shot in the left thigh. He was a faithful soldier and is a charter member of Duro Post.

W. A. Johnson, born in Lewis county in 1842, enlisting August 11, 1862. He is an honored member of Duro Post, was a good soldier, and did splendid service in the field; was wounded in the hand at Salem Church. He was always at his post, a most companionable soldier and gentleman, and is at the present time Chaplain of the Post.

Thomas Jenks was born at Burlington, N. Y., in 1812; enlisted Sept. 6, 1862, in Co. H, 152d Regt. N. Y. Vols.; is an honored citizen of Hartwick and a worthy member of Duro Post. Although advanced in years he takes a lively interest in the G. A. R. He did good service for the right, and recalls with pleasure the many scenes and incidents of camp life during his service.

Samuel Drew, born in Chenango county in 1836; educated in Otsego county, and enlisted, Oct. 10, 1861, in Co. E, 6th N. Y. Cavalry; mustered in at Staten Island, Oct. 10, 1861. He did splendid service with his regiment; was wounded near Barryville during Sheridan's retreat in the Shenandoah, Sept. 17, 1864; sent to hospital at Arlington Heights, thence to Baltimore, Philadelphia and Albany, and in February transferred to the Third Veteran Reserve Corps; participating in the battles of Antietam, Gettysburg and Chancellorsville. Discharged, Sept. 12, 1865. Located at Hartwick in 1877. He joined Duro Post as a charter member, and at the present time is Junior Vice Commander. He is now residing at Hartwick with his family, wife and daughter, aged 16.

Abel Wrigley, born in England in 1842, coming to America in 1848, and educated in Wyoming county, Pa. He enlisted Sept. 15, 1862, as First Corporal in Julius P. Skinner's Independent Co., State of Pa. Was discharged Sept. 23, 1862; located at Hartwick in April, 1891, and joined Duro Post, July 16, 1892. He is at the present time pastor of the Methodist Episcopal church at Hartwick, where he is residing with his family, a wife, four daughters and son; one daughter, aged 28, is residing at Deposit, N. Y.

Addison Gilbert was born at Laurens, Otsego county, N. Y., in 1829. He enlisted in July, 1863, in Co. E, 2d

H. O. BRANCH,

Fine Merchant Tailoring

— AND DEALER IN —

Stationery and School Supplies.

Suits Overcoats and Trousers Made to Order in the Latest Styles.

Main Street, Post Office Building,
HARTWICK, N. Y.

E. N. HIGBIE,

DEALER IN

FINE FURNITURE

Parlor and Chamber Suites, Spring Beds, Mattresses, &c.

Funeral Director & Furnisher
AND PRACTICAL EMBALMER.

Hartwick, Otsego County, N. Y.

N. Y. H. A. He was a good soldier, with a brave regiment, doing splendid service at Tolopotomy Creek, North Anna, Cold Harbor, at Hatch's Run and Five Forks. He is now an honored member of Duro Post, 653.

James Simmons, born in Delaware county, Feb. 22, 1845, and enlisted Jan. 3, 1861, as a private in Co. I, 89th N. Y. V., going to Elmira and thence to Washington. Sick with fever, and sent to hospital January 14, 1862; rejoined his regiment in June, 1862, at Roanoke Island, N. C. His regiment is that of this famous regiment, participating in all battles, marches and skirmishes in which they were engaged. After the battle at Chapin's farm he was detatched from the regiment and placed on duty as a sharp-shooter, where he remained until discharged, Aug. 12, 1865, participating in the battles at Kingston, Whitehall, Goldsboro, seige of Washington, N. C., seige of Sulfolk, Quaker Bridge, Great Swamp, Bachelor Creek, Drewry's Bluff, Bermuda Hundred, Cold Harbor, Petersburg, June 15, Mine Explosion, Petersburg, Trenches, Chapin's Farm, Fair Oaks, and Fall of Richmond. Always at his post, displaying great courage. Located at Hartwick in 1885; joined Duro Post as a charter member, and is at the present time Adjutant of the Post. Resides at Hartwick with his family, wife, daughter, aged 18, and two sons, aged 16 and 10.

Asel McTice, born in St. Lawrence county in 1832; enlisted Dec. 14, 1863, as a private in the 14th N. Y. H. A. His record is that of his regiment; garrisoned the forts in New York harbor until April 23, 1864; ordered to the front, joining the 9th Corps at Warrenton, Va., and started, May 2, 1864, for the Rapidan. The regiment was in line at the Wilderness and engaged at Spotsylvania, and at Cold Harbor suffered heavily. At Petersburg,

H. C. BUNN,

DEALER IN

Dry Goods, Groceries,

Hats, Caps, Boots, Shoes & Ready-made Clothing.

Farm Produce taken in Exchange for Goods.

Mount Vision, Otsego Co., N. Y.

G. M. AUGUR,

DEALER IN

HEAVY AND SHELF HARDWARE,

AND HOUSE FURNISHING GOODS.

Stoves and Ranges.

REPAIRING NEATLY DONE,

Hartwick, Otsego County, N. Y.

June 17, 1864, the 14th distinguished itself by its brilliant and successful charge on the works at Petersburg. At the mine explosion the regiment was selected to lead the assault at the crater, and was the first to plant its colors on the enemy's works, where it captured a Confederate flag. Participated in battles at North Anna, Va., Bethesda Church, Cold Harbor, Weldon Railroad and the fall of Petersburg. Discharged in June, 1865. Moved to Hartwick in 1880, and joined Duro Post as a charter member. Resides in Hartwick, N. Y., and is at the present time Surgeon of the Post.

Milton Higbie, Second Lieutenant in Bates Battery, was a brave soldier and scholar; he was born in the town of Exeter, July 12, 1833. No officer or enlisted man ever served his term with more fidelity than did Lieutenant Higbie. After his discharge returned to Exeter and died, Nov. 7, 1881, and was buried in the Hartwick cemetery. He left a devoted wife and son, Edgar N., now residing at Hartwick, N. Y.

Allen Cotton, born in Jefferson county in 1842, and enlisted as a private in Co. K, 10th N. Y. H. A., Feb. 26, 1864, serving faithfully with his regiment until discharged. Joined Duro Post, and is at the present time Quartermaster Sergeant.

Cornelius Bird, born in 1846, and enlisting Aug. 3, 1864, in Co. H, 20th Regulars. He was a good soldier and entitled to the honors of his regiment. Is an active member and Sergeant Major of Duro Post, Hartwick, N. Y.

G. W. Murdock, the present efficient Quartermaster of the Post, was born in August, 1842. Enlisted in September 1862, in Co. G, 17th N. Y. Vols. He left home and friends to fight the battles of his country, and is now nearly blind as the result of an explosion while at the front. He is a charter member of Duro Post, 653.

Though not a member, the Post has a warm friend in the person of Rev. H. H. Fisher, of Hartwick, N. Y. He is at all times and on all occasions at the Post's command. He is a fluent speaker, and in the hour of his country's trial sent hot shot from the rostrum to the ears of rebel sympathizers.

POST OFFICERS.

Lester W. Murdock	Commander.
William Blanchard	Senior Vice Commander.
Samuel Drew	Junior Vice Commander.
James Simmons	Adjutant.
G. W. Murdock	Quartermaster.
Asel McTice	Surgeon.
Emmet Irons	Officer of the Day.
Menzo Bishop	Officer of the Guard.
W. A. Johnson	Chaplain.
Cornelius Bird	Sergeant Major.

PAST COMMANDERS.

Lester W. Murdock.

LIST OF MEMBERS.

Blanchard, William	K, 114 N. Y. V.
Bird Cornelius	H, 20 Regular
Colton, Allen	K, 10 N. Y. H. A.
Card, Tabor	A, 1 N. Y. L. A.
Drew, Samuel	E, 6 N. Y. C.
Gilbert, Addison	E, 2 N. Y. H. A.
Holdridge, William	B, 9th H. A.

Irons, Emmet M..E, 121 N. Y. V.
Jenks, Thomas...H, 152 N. Y. V.
Johnson, William A.......................................F, 121 N. Y. V.
Murdock, Lester W..E, 121 N. Y. V.
Murdock, G. W..G, 17 N. Y. V.
McTice, Asel...14 N. Y. H. A.
Simmons, James..I, 89 N. Y. V.
Wrigley, Abel................................Ind. Co., Penn. Inf.

GRAVES DECORATED BY DURO POST.

Alger. Chester..E, 121 N. Y. V.
Clark, ———..
Higbie Milton...Bates' Battery
Luce, Harvey...
Pickens, Edwin...H, 152 N. Y. V.
Rinders, George..121 N. Y. V.
Wicks, James..
Westcott, ———...
Walker, Ripley...War of 1812.

SISSON & JOYCE,
FURNITURE ✥ AND ✥ UNDERTAKING,
PICTURE FRAMES
—AND—
UPHOLSTERY GOODS.
305 MAIN ST., NORTH BLOCK, UNADILLA, N. Y.

This business was established in 1890 by F. M. Sisson and F. J. Joyce, and since that time they have experienced great prosperity, and built up the handsome trade they now enjoy. It is one of the most progressive business houses in Otsego county. They take a great pride in carrying a modern and attractive stock. Here you can get the same styles, and qualities, in all kinds of furniture and upholstery goods at much lower prices than in larger cities. Their store rooms occupy three floors, 24x100 feet, and is thoroughly stocked with parlor and chamber suits, fancy chairs of all descriptions, stands, easels, sideboards, spring beds and mattresses, extension and centre tables.

The shop is located in the rear of the store ; here all kinds of repairing and upholstering is done on short notice and reasonable terms.

The members of the firm are genial, affable gentlemen and always make it pleasant and agreeable for their numerous patrons, and **for all who may favor them with a visit.**

L. C. Turner Post, No. 26,

COOPERSTOWN, N. Y.

Regular Meetings Every Wednesday Evening at G. A. R Hall.

THE POST was organized and mustered into the Department of New York, May 26, 1878. At the first meeting of the Post Hon. Andrew Davidson was chosen Commander. He was born at Morebattle, Roxburyshire, Scotland, February 12, 1840, coming to America, and enlisting at Cooperstown, N. Y., in July, 1862, in Co. E, 121st Regiment, N. Y. V., and was promoted to sergeant at the organization of the regiment at Herkimer, Aug. 23, 1862. The regiment joined Gen. McClellan's army, then in Maryland. After the battles of Fredericksburg, Maryland Heights and Salem Church was promoted to sergeant-major; was severely wounded at Salem Church, May 3, 1863, and sent to the hospital; rejoined the regiment at Warrentown, Va.; he was commissioned by Abraham Lincoln, in 1864, as First Lieutenant, and assigned to the 30th Regiment, U. S. Colored Troops, and appointed Adjutant of the Regiment. He was with Colonel Bates at the head of the regiment as they led the Colored Division in its charge to blow up the fort at Petersburg, Va., July 30, 1864; promoted to Captain and appointed aide de camp to General Delivan Bates, and subsequently as Assistant Adjutant General on his staff; he was afterward appointed by General Ruger, commanding Department of North Carolina, Assistant Adjutant General and Acting

C. R. BURCH,
JEWELER,

COOPERSTOWN, N. Y.

Watches, Clocks, Jewelry, Sterling Silver and Silver Plated ware. Fancy Goods.

WATCHES, CLOCKS AND JEWELRY NEATLY REPAIRED.

Central Shoe Store,

OPPOSITE CENTRAL HOTEL.
COOPERSTOWN, N. Y.

I carry the largest stock of Ladies', Misses' and Childrens'

FOOTWEAR

To be found in this County, at prices which Defy Competition.

I am sole agent for the Celebrated Snag Proof Rubber Boots.

Terms Strictly Cash. **W. H. BUNDY.**

Assistant Inspector General of the eastern division of North Carolina; was assigned to the staff of General Chas. J. Payne, commanding the district. Was mustered out, after three years of active service. When the war broke out he had just finished (at Cooperstown) a preparatory course, expecting to enter Hamilton College. After his discharge he returned to Cooperstown, studied law and was admitted to the Bar. Soon afterward he became the proprietor of The Otsego Republican, an influential family and political newspaper. He is a staunch Republican and an active member of that party; has served as chairman of the county committee and a member of the State committee; represented the 23d district in the State Senate during 1884 and 1885. He is a prominent member of the Presbyterian Church, the G. A. R., Loyal Legion and Masons. Was a delegate to the National Encampment, G. A. R., at Detroit, and placed in nomination John M. Palmer, the present Commander. He was appointed in March, First Deputy Commissioner of Pensions, to succeed Hiram Smith, Jr., of Missouri. The Post, under his administration, soon became one of prominence in the Department.

Reuben H. Bates, the present Commander, was born in Dutchess county, Aug. 20, 1827. When a boy he came to Otsego county and was educated at Middlefield. He enlisted in August, 1862, as a private Co. G., 121st N. Y. Vols.; his record is that of his regiment, which was one of the bravest in the army; he participated in more than twenty of the bloodiest battles of the war; was taken prisoner at Salem Church, May 6, 1863, and sent to Bell Island; remained fourteen days, was parolled and sent to Annapolis, then to Alexandria and to Camp Convalescent, where he remained four weeks, and joined his regiment at Warrentown Junction. Discharged at Hall's Hill,

June 25, 1865. Returned to Cooperstown. Is a charter member of Turner Post; has served as Chaplain, Adjutant, Senior and Junior Vice, and elected Commander for the unexpired term, made vacant by the resignation of Andrew Davidson, and in December, 1891, again elected for the year 1892. Although living nearly two miles from the place of meeting, he has missed but three meetings during his term. He is now residing at Cooperstown with his family, wife and daughter, aged 19; a son is in the employ of the United States Express Company, running between Scranton and Elmira.

J. F. Reustle was born in Germany, in December, 1847. Educated in Germany, coming to America in 1862. Locating at Cooperstown, was employed as a clerk. In 1864, went to New Jersey, and in September of the same year enlisted in Co. C, 7th N. J. V., when only 16 years old, going to the front and joining the 3d Brigade, 3d Division, 26th Corps. Engaged in the battles at Hatch's Run, Popular Spring, and near Petersburg. Discharged in July, 1865; returned to Cooperstown and was employed as clerk in a hardware store for fourteen years; in 1880 went into the dry and fancy goods business. Joined the Post as a charter member; served as Officer of the Day, and was elected Commander for the year 1879. Many comrades of the 152d and 121st will recall with pleasure the re-union at Cooperstown, N. Y., in 1890, its great success being largely due to his personal efforts.

The Post was named for the distinguished scholar and former citizen of Cooperstown, L. C. Turner, born at Claremont, N. H., Oct. 15, 1806; he was a lawyer by profession; previous to taking up his residence in Cooperstown he had traveled extensively in England and on the Continent. He was a gentleman of rare endowments socially, and a racy, graceful and ready writer; as a companion, Judge Turner was one of the most charming of men; at one time taking a deep interest in politics; he was twice elected to the bench of Otsego county, and as a judge his career was marked with judgment and talent. He resigned the judgeship, having been selected by Secretary of War Edwin M. Stanton, to take the position of Judge Advocate, the Secretary having known the Judge intimately when residing in this State. The confidential relations existing between Secretary Stanton and Judge Turner made the latter intimately conversant with the secret service of the department, and had he kept a diary it would have contained the most interesting portion of the history of the War. The life of Judge Turner was so interesting as to be even romantic. His early years was a struggle with the world, but a generous disposition, winning manners, talent of a high order, reasonable, and an ambition that never allowed an obstacle to obstruct his path, gained for him a liberal education at Dartmouth and Union, which enabled him to acquire a profession. He died at Washington, D. C., March 13, 1867, aged sixty years and six months, leaving a widow, a daughter, Mrs. Randolph, and a son, Theo. C. Turner, now cashier of the First National Bank at Cooperstown.

Erie S. Collar, born in 1834, in the City of New York, and enlisted Sept. 19, 1863, in Co. D, 146th N. Y. V.; was wounded at Bethesda Church, June 2, 1864, losing his right arm; was captured and sent to Richmond to the hospital, where he remained until parolled and sent to provost camp at Annapolis, and soon after transferred to hospital corner Broad and Cherry streets, and discharged May 28, 1865. Located at Cooperstown and joined Turner Post; served as Quartermaster for several years. He is residing at Cooperstown with his family, wife, two sons and two daughters.

H. C. Richmond, born at Oneonta, N. Y., April 21, 1847. Educated at the common schools, and enlisted in January, 1864, in Co. E, 2d N. Y. H. A. Ordered to New York to Fort Schuyler, and aboard the boat Admiral Dupont for Fortress Monroe, March 10, 1864; at Alexandria, March 12, and to Arlington Heights March 13; joined his regiment at Fort Bennett, Va., to Alexandria, and aboard transports for Aqua Creek, Bell Plain Landing, on the Potomac, and May 14, to Fredericksburg, joining the army on the 18th of May at Spotsylvania, and under fire but not engaged; 19th of May engaged in battle, the rebels attempting to capture the wagon train; thence to Toloptomy Creek, North Anna and Cold Harbor to Petersburg, and engaged in battle June 16, and wounded June 17; sent to hospital and joined regiment in front of Petersburg, Oct. 17; engaged in second battle at Hatch's Run, Dec. 9, 1864, Five Forks, April 6, and Round Fort, April 7, 1865. Was with the regiment until they were discharged, Sept. 18, 1865. Was charter member and Past Commander of Olcott Post, and joined Turner Post by transfer card, in 1888; has served as Officer of the Day, and elected Adjutant for the years 1890-91-92.

Michael Little was born in Ireland in 1837, and came to America in 1857, locating at Herkimer, N. Y. In 1860 he moved to Cooperstown, and enlisted, Oct. 3, 1863, in Co. K, 20 N. Y. C. Ordered to Washington, then to Camp Stoneman, to Camp Getty; remained three months, then to Suffolk; engaged in battle at Black Water, Deep Bottom, Dansville to Winchester. Discharged July 16, 1865. Returned to Cooperstown, joined Post in 1886, served as Officer of the Guard for three years, and is now Quartermaster of the Post. Resides in Cooperstown with wife and daughter, aged 35, and two sons, ages 23 and 13.

Thomas T. Collar, born in England, March 15, 1826,

coming to America and locating at Cooperstown in October, 1849. Enlisted June 20, 1863, at the Bay Hia, coast of Brazil, S. A., and assigned to service on board the U. S. ship Onward. Was discharged at Brooklyn, N. Y., in June, 1865, and returned to Cooperstown, joined the Post in April, 1882, and is now Surgeon of the Post. Resides in Cooperstown, his family consisting of wife, three daughters and one son.

John A. Lakin was born in Utica, N. Y., April 8, 1838; was educated in New York, and enlisted Aug. 3, 1864, in Co. A, 91st N. Y. Vols. Ordered to Fort McHenry, Baltimore, then to City Point; in the spring of 1865 was with Sheridan; engaged in first and second battles at Hatch's Run, Gravely Run, Five Forks and in skirmishes to Appomatox. Discharged from service; located at Cooperstown in 1870, and joined Post in 1887; has served as Quartermaster Sergeant, Sergeant Major, and is at the present time Junior Vice Commander of the Post.

POST OFFICERS.

R. H. Bates.....................Commander.
Gardner Hollis.................Senior Vice Commander.
J. A. Lakin....................Junior Vice Commander.
H. C. Richmond.................Adjutant.
Michael Little.................Quartermaster.
Thomas Collar..................Surgeon.
F. Hubbel......................Chaplain.
John Lasher....................Officer of the Day.

PAST COMMANDERS.

Andrew Davidson,   Henry Wood,   Fred. Reustle,
                   W. B. Flanigan.

LIST OF MEMBERS.

Arnold, A. E................................A, 1 N. Y. A.

Fredk. Schneider,

Cooperstown
Bakery & Confectionery

(Opposite Hotel Fenimore)

COR. MAIN AND CHESTNUT STREETS.

THE FINEST ESTABLISHMENT OF ITS KIND IN OTSEGO COUNTY.

EVERYTHING IN THE BAKERY AND CONFECTIONERY LINE, ICE CREAM, ETC.

PARTIES, CHURCHES AND WEDDINGS SUPPLIED.

PRICES REASONABLE.   FINEST GOODS.

H. W. THAYER, PROPRIETOR,

Cooperstown Laundry

AND

Carpet Cleaning Works,

SUSQUEHANNA STREET. - COOPERSTOWN, N. Y.

❋ ❋ ❋ ❋ ❋ ❋ ❋ ❋

WORK CALLED FOR AND DELIVERED IN THE VILLAGE.

Adsit, James...I, 144 N. Y.
Bates, R. H..G, 121 N. Y.
Best. Peter...A, 176 N. Y.
Bingham, Thomas..45 N. Y.
Brown, Lorin...B, 77 N. Y.
Butts, Elijah...F, 121 N. Y.
Becker, George..D, 5 N Y. C.
Bliss, Sanford T..E, 5 Iowa Cav.
Barret, Edward..169 N. Y.
Bingham, Samuel W......................................66 N. Y.
Baldwin, L. W..152 N Y.
Bullis, Albert...H, 121 N. Y.
Bailey. D. W..E, 121 N. Y.
Blunk, John..D, 6 Mich
Bailey, Albert...E, 121 N. Y.
Clark, James F...E, 121 N. Y
Collar, Erie S...D, 146 N. Y.
Camp, W. H H..E, 2 Vt. Vols.
Crandall, Lucius..G, 114 N. Y.
Clark, A. F..A, 1 N. Y. A.
Collar. T. T...U. S. Steamer Onward.
Clark, Frank A...U. S. Steamer Galena.
Davis, Charles L.........................
Dickinson, Allen..E, 2 N. Y, A.
Deits, Michael..C, 26 N. Y.
Dyer, E. H..F, 121 N. Y.
Doubleday, Thomas M..................................68 N. Y.
Davidson, Andrew D....................................E, 121 N. Y.
Earing, Alfred..G, 3 N. Y.
Elwood Amenzo W......................................D, 121 N. Y.
Freeland, H. E...C. 6 N. Y. A.
Frech, Allison..F, 14 Res. Corps.
Flanigan, William B....................................G, 24 Mich.
Gardner Addison..Bat. K, 3 N. Y. L. A.
Gardner, Hollis..G, 24 N. Y.

Gould Elery C................................D, 6 N. Y. C.
Hiller, W. H ....15 N. Y. A.
Hills E Delivan...........................G, 221 N. Y.
Hardson, C R..............................35 N. Y.
Hyde, George S...........................1 N. Y L. A.
Henry. W. H..............................D, 14 Reg,
Hearn, Thomes H........................I 144 N. Y.
Henderson Robert........................I, 1 N. Y.
House, Charles B........................M, 3 N. Y. L. A.
Ingalls, H. E.............................K, 4 N. Y.
Jarvis, Fred. T...........................C, 152 N. Y.
Judson, J. H..............................Record not given.
Jones, L. L...............................A, 1 N. Y. L A.
Jarvis, Frank G..........................G, 3 N. Y. C.
Kellogg, William J......................I, 152 N. Y.
Kendell, U B............................H, 152 N. Y.
Keough, Mortimer.......................L, 2 N Y.
Lasher, John C..........................I, 152 N. Y.
Lakin, John A...........................A, 91 N. Y.
Lindsey, W. F...........................K, 43 N. Y.
Little. M ....K, 30 N. Y. C.
Markel, E. N............................H, 121 N. Y.
Mandeville Luke........................A, 152 N. Y.
Morton, William H.....................G, 10 Mich.
Murphy, William........................E, 123 N. Y.
Miller, Edwin...........................3 N. Y. L. A.
McIntyre, D............................K, 3 U S. Art.; 43 N. Y.
Meriels C. N...........................I, 121 N. Y.
Niles, D. C.............................K, 43 N. Y.
Parish, Jeremiah........................H, 152 N. Y.
Perry, H L ....F, 121 N. Y.
Platts, A. G.............................A, 43 N. Y.
Reustle, J. Fred........................C, 7 N. Y.
Spencer, William G....................A, 43 N. Y.
Shute Robert...........................B, 152 N. Y.

Sherwood, George E.....................D, 14 Reg.
Shillits, John..............................F, 5 N. Y. C.
Topping, J. P............................A, 23 N. Y.
Thayer, Julius B.........................K, 75 N. Y.
Van Ort, Adam..........................K, 76 N. Y.
Van Court, D. P.........................G, 34 N. Y.
Wicks, John H...........................H, 152 N. Y.
Wicks, J. R...............................B, 4 N. Y. C.
Wood, John T...........................E, 121 N. Y.
Walker, Henry B........................E, 121 N. Y.
Wood, Henry............................E, 121 N. Y.
Walradt, William........................G, 91 N. Y.
Yomans, Joseph........................G, 1 N. Y. Eng.

In Memoriam.

Ira Wright................................F, 121 N. Y.
Israel l'arshall...........................B, 2 N. Y. H. A.
James Bowmaker......................G, 152 N. Y.
Henry E. Palmer.......................H, 121 N. Y,
Silas W. Pierce.........................E, 121 N. Y.
Charles Compton......................E, 121 N. Y.
L. Secoy.................................Record Unknown

www.ingramcontent.com/pod-product-compliance
Lightning Source LLC
Chambersburg PA
CBHW032007230426
43672CB00010B/2280